Aspects of modern socio

THE SOCIAL STRU MODERN BRITAIN

GENERAL EDITORS

John Barron Mays
Eleanor Rathbone Professor of Sociology,
University of Liverpool

Maurice Craft
Professor of Education,
University of Nottingham

ASPECTS OF MODERN SOCIOLOGY

General Editors

John Barron Mays Professor of Sociology, University of Liverpool
Maurice Craft Professor of Education, University of Nottingham

This Longman library of texts in modern sociology consists of three Series, and includes the following titles:

THE SOCIAL STRUCTURE OF MODERN BRITAIN

The family
Mary Farmer
formerly University of Liverpool

The political structure
Grace Jones
Chester College
of Higher Education

Population
Prof. R.K. Kelsall
University of Sheffield

Education
Ronald King
University of Exeter

The welfare state
Prof. David Marsh
University of Nottingham

Crime and its treatment
Prof. John Barron Mays
University of Liverpool

Structures and processes of urban life
Prof. R. E. Pahl
University of Kent
R. Flynn
University of Salford
N. H. Buck
University of Kent

The working class
Kenneth Roberts
University of Liverpool

The middle class
Roger King
Huddersfield Polytechnic
and
John Raynor
The Open University

Leisure
Kenneth Roberts
University of Liverpool

The mass media
Peter Golding
University of Leicester

Rural life
Gwyn Jones
University of Reading

Mental illness
Bernard Ineichen
University of Bristol

The economic structure
Prof. Cedric Sandford
University of Bath

SOCIAL PROCESSES

Communication
Prof. Denis McQuail
University of Amsterdam

Stratification
Prof. R. K. Kelsall
University of Sheffield
and
H. Kelsall

Socialisation
Graham White
University of Liverpool

Social Conflict
Prof. John Rex
University of Aston

Forthcoming titles will include:

Migration
Prof. J. A. Jackson
University of Dublin

SOCIAL RESEARCH

The Limitations of Social Research
Prof. M. D. Shipman
University of Warwick

The Philosophy of Social Research
John Hughes
University of Lancaster

Data Collection in Context
Stephen Ackroyd
and
John Hughes
University of Lancaster

BY THE SAME AUTHOR (R. E. PAHL)
Urbs in Rure (*1965*)
Readings in Urban Sociology (*Ed.*) (*1968*)
Whose City? (*1975*)

Structures and Processes of Urban Life

R. E. PAHL M.A., Ph. D.
Professor of Sociology
University of Kent

R. FLYNN B.A., M.A.
Lecturer in Sociology
University of Salford

N. H. BUCK B.A., Ph. D.
Honorary Research Fellow
University of Kent

Second edition

Longman London and New York

Longman Group Limited
Longman House, Burnt Mill, Harlow
Essex CM20 2JE, England
Associated companies throughout the world

*Published in the United States of America
by Longman Inc., New York*

© Longman Group Limited 1970, 1983

First published as Patterns of Urban Life, 1970

British Library Cataloguing in Publication Data
Pahl, R. E.
  Structures and processes of urban life. – (Aspects of modern sociology.
  The social structure of modern Britain)
  1. City and town life – Great Britain
  2. Great Britain – Social life and customs
  I. Title   II. Flynn, R.   III. Buck, N. H.   IV. Series

  941′.00973′2   HT133

  ISBN 0-582-29543-2

Library of Congress Cataloging in Publication Data
Pahl, R. E. (Raymond Edward), 1935–
  Structures and processes of urban life.

  (Aspects of modern sociology. The Social structure of modern Britain)
  Rev. ed. of: Patterns of urban life. 1970.
  Bibliography: p. 150
  Includes index.
  1. Cities and towns – Great Britain.
2. Great Britain – Social conditions. 3. Urban economics.
I. Flynn, R. (Robert), 1951–
II. Buck, N. H., 1953–   III. Title.   IV. Series: Aspects of
modern sociology. Social structure of modern Britain.
HT133.P34   1983   307.7′64′0941   82–13093 ISBN 0-582-29543-2

Set in 10/12pt Linotron 202 Plantin
Printed in Singapore by
Huntsmen Offset Printing Pte Ltd.

CONTENTS

EDITORS' PREFACE

This series has been designed to meet the needs of students following a variety of academic and professional courses in universities, polytechnics, colleges of higher education, colleges of education, and colleges of further education. Although principally of interest to social scientists, the series does not attempt a comprehensive treatment of the whole field of sociology, but concentrates on the social structure of modern Britain which forms a central feature of most such tertiary level courses in this country. Its purpose is to offer an analysis of our contemporary society through the study of basic demographic, ideological and structural features, and the examination of such major social institutions as the family, education, the economic and political structure and religion. The aim has been to produce a series of introductory texts which will in combination form the basis for a sustained course of study, but each volume has been designed as a single whole and can be read in its own right.

We hope that the topics covered in the series will prove attractive to a wide reading public and that, in addition to students, others who wish to know more than is readily available about the nature and structure of their own society will find them of interest.

John Barron Mays
Maurice Craft

FOREWORD

The first edition of this book, entitled *Patterns of Urban Life*, was written in 1969 and published a year later. This book is more than a new edition: it is in every respect a new book. Chapters 1 and 2 and parts of Chapter 3 are much the same, but all the rest is completely new and the style of argument is quite different from the previous edition.

My two co-authors are both former post-graduate students at the University of Kent at Canterbury and each has had a research grant from the Social Science Research Council. Rob Flynn studied aspects of urban managerialism and Nick Buck worked on the historical approach to occupational communities. Thus it was not difficult for us to work together as we all share a common approach. This book follows directly from the experience of teaching and research at the University of Kent during the past decade. We have all worked on all the chapters and revised each other's drafts, but inevitably there has been some division of labour. Rob Flynn was responsible for first drafts of Chapters 4, 5 and 6 and Nick Buck drafted the revisions in Chapters 2 and 3 and the final draft of Chapter 8, as well as later drafts of the others. I was responsible for the overall planning and shaping of the book in its new guise and for the new Chapters 7 and 9. Without such a programme of friendly collaboration, this book would not have been possible. We are all very grateful to Jane Dennett for meticulous typing of the manuscript, despite a particularly heavy burden of other work.

R. E. Pahl

ACKNOWLEDGEMENTS

We are indebted to the following for permission to reproduce copyright material:

the Controller of Her Majesty's Stationery Office for our Table 6.1; Institute of Historical Research, University of London for our Table 1.1; Oxford University Press for our Fig. 3.2; University of Chicago Press for our Fig. 3.1 from (Park, Burgess & Mackenzie 1925); University of Michigan Press for our Tables 1.2 and 1.3 from (Thrupp 1948); University of North Carolina, Institute for Social Science for our Figs 3.3 and 3.4 from pp. 101 and 105 (Boal, Murray & Poole 1976).

1

THE ORIGINS AND GROWTH OF PRE-INDUSTRIAL URBANISM IN BRITAIN

There has been some form of urban life in Britain for nearly 2,000 years. According to almost any criterion, Britain is now among the most urbanised two or three nations in the world. Sociologists are interested not so much in the physical growth of towns and cities and not, even, in the proportionate increase of the population living in areas designated as urban, but rather in the changing patterns of social relationships which may develop in urban areas. This analytical distinction between the physical situation and social relationships gives rise to certain difficulties and confusion in modern Britain, which, in many respects, may be considered to be completely urbanised in the sociological sense. These difficulties were much less apparent during the early period of the development of urban life and institutions in Britain or in Western Europe generally. The town or city, even without its wall, rampart or ditch, appeared clearly separate and distinguishable from the country.

In this chapter we shall first consider the early colonisation and urbanisation of tribal Britain by a large bureaucratically organised and urban-based imperial power. Then, using the rather slender historical material available, we shall consider urban life and social institutions in two English pre-industrial cities, York and London. This will be related to the more general sociological work of the distinguished German sociologist Max Weber, who wrote one of the pioneer works in urban sociology early in this century. More recently, the American sociologist Gideon Sjoberg has written on pre-industrial cities and we shall also consider his contribution. It should be stressed that we are not so much concerned with telling a story, inferring that what comes before is directly related to what follows; rather, we are concerned with specifically sociological themes, which may be discussed in the light of the available historical evidence. The main focus is on social institutions and social relationships.

The beginnings of urban society and urban ideologies

Tribal Britain was administered from fortified camps which some people have described as towns. However, it was the conquest and colonisation by the Roman legionaries and administrators that introduced cities to Britain. In many ways the Roman Empire was the creation of the city and Roman intellectuals had much the same ambivalent attitudes towards urbanism as contemporary intellectuals (Lowenstein 1965).

Many authors in ancient Rome complained of the noise, the traffic and the crowds. Horace complained of 'that bit of Hell/Known as big city life', and Martial complained of the transience or superficiality of certain urban social relationships – 'in all the city there is no man who is so near and yet so far from me' as his own next-door neighbour. The jaded satirists not only deplored the physical form and pattern of urban life, but also the source of income of the rich; Horace wrote:

> Some men derive their income from government contracts;
> Some hunt down rich widows, with fruit and glazed candy;
> Some cast their nets for old men to put in their fishponds;
> Some people's capital keeps on growing, kept growing
> By interest (fostered by time, just like a tree).

In the sophisticated city, life was claimed to be vile and corrupt, whereas the good life could be lived in the country: after all, as Varro put it – 'God made the country and man made the town'. Typically, the rich got the best of both worlds: 'Whenever worn out with worry, I wish to sleep, I go to my villa', remarked Martial, and Pliny was obliged to commute to peace at his villa, 'but seventeen miles distant from Rome; so that having finished your affairs in town, you can spend the night here after completing a full working day'. Yet there were, of course, dissenting voices; Cicero did not enjoy life in the country:

> I cannot discribe how ardently I long for town, how hard I find it to bear the stupidity of life here.

Even Horace makes one of his characters in his *Satires* laugh at him:

At Rome, you yearn
For the country, but once in the sticks, you praise to high heaven
The far off city, you nitwit.

These views are not confined to the Romans. For as long as there has been a contrast between town and country, writers have seen this as one of the central divisions in society. The attitudes have been complex. The arcadian peace and beauty of the country has been contrasted with the dirt and corruption of the city. The dynamism and civilisation of the city has been contrasted with the idiocy of rural life. A major contribution to the understanding of this question has been made by Raymond Williams's book, *The Country and the City* (1973). In it he explores the attitudes to country and city in English literature from the sixteenth century to the present. Above all, he shows the potency of the two images. He argues that the 'contrast between the country and the city is one of the major forms in which we became conscious of a central part of our experience and of the crises of our society'.

Although urban life was the basis of the ancient Mediterranean civilisations, it was not easy to establish it in tribal parts of the Empire, like Britain. The Romans adopted a policy of creating what French geographers have described in once French-occupied Africa as binocular towns – the Roman town was built adjoining the tribal camp. This system had the advantage of close proximity to the old tribal aristocracy who were then responsible for levying local taxes; the unit of administration was based on the existing tribal area and the urban network became the main source of British Romanisation. However, most Roman towns were simply military camps and only five British towns had a status which enabled their inhabitants to have the rights of Roman citizenship. One of these, Verulamium (St Albans), may have been a *municipium*, which would have merited its own charter and constitution. Archaeological evidence has shown that Verulamium certainly had pretensions to grandeur. At the peak of its prosperity there were large triumphal arches, temples, an open air theatre and a forum with large centrally heated houses built in a prosperous colonial style in brick and tile. In his report on excavations at Verulamium, S. S. Frere suggested that the more wealthy men of the Catuvellauni tribe invested their money in blocks of shops fronting Watling Street.

Acculturation followed urban development: Tacitus describes how Agricola provided educational facilities for the sons of tribal chiefs so that 'in place of distaste for the Latin language came a passion to command it. In the same way, our national dress came into favour and the toga was everywhere to be seen. And so the Britons were gradually led on to the amenities that make vice agreeable – arcades, baths and sumptuous banquets. They spoke of such novelties as "civilisation", when really they were only a feature of enslavement' (Tacitus p. 72).

It is difficult to believe that this period of some 300 years of urbanisation and Romanisation did not have some lasting effects. Substantial villas were built in the countryside by the new gentry, with masonry footings, mosaic floors, bath-houses, heated rooms, and glazed windows. Even if towns declined between the Saxon invasions and the Norman conquest, a more sophisticated urban style may have continued amongst a scattered Romano-British population, which could have provided the basis for the merchant-trader class which appeared in the eighth and ninth centuries. And the withdrawal of the Roman legions in the fifth century may not have led to quite the eclipse of urban life that some historians have claimed. As Professor Edward Miller (1961) put it: 'There seems, in fact, every reason to believe that seventh-century townsmen were fully conscious of the origins of the Roman monuments around them. In York, the massive walls and columns of the earlier culture . . . must have inspired even farmer and artisan with some sense of urban community.' York maintained a strong urban tradition from the fifth to the tenth centuries. Canterbury also maintained its urban tradition and as early as the ninth century there is reference to a Cnihtengild – an organisation for a defined section of the town, although who the Cnihts of Canterbury were is not clear. These early urban voluntary organisations are fore-runners of the medieval guilds. Regulations for a thegns' guild at Cambridge are mainly concerned with the rituals connected with the blood feud, but there is also some concern with funeral dues, the transport of a member's body if he is taken ill or dies outside the district, and so on.

It is likely that in some English urban centres, trade and industry carried on through the Dark Ages. Nevertheless, there is dispute among historians whether, apart from London and one or two other places, there were any real towns in Anglo-Saxon England. Certainly, many burghs were closely integrated into the rural economy with little that could be described as distinctly urban in any sociological sense. However, evidence is accumulating of quite considerable urban development. For example, in the ninth and tenth centuries, the Anglo-Danish town of Thetford developed a broad industrial and trading structure. Metal smiths worked iron and copper and there was a flourishing woollen and pottery industry. Trade extended all over eastern England and to the Continent. Other inhabitants of the town were farmers providing the food for the industrial workers. The site of the town extended for about a mile along the Little Ouse valley and stretched inland for half a mile. At the time of the Domestic Survey in 1086, Thetford was an administrative and commercial centre comparable with Norwich or Oxford and had maybe 4,000 or 5,000 inhabitants. York probably had more than 8,000 inhabitants and was divided into smaller units known as 'shires'. London probably had 12,000 inhabitants, though Domesday evidence is lacking. At the end of the eleventh century, perhaps a tenth of England's population lived permanently in towns, and even if many of these towns' inhabitants were farmers, there was a substantial minority of urban Englishmen, legally and politically distinct and apart from the manorial structure.

However, the early urbanisation of Britain by the Romans and merchants is obscure, owing to the lack of documentary evidence. It is nonetheless possible that if a tenth of the population did live permanently in towns by the end of the eleventh century, then England was more urbanised than Africa has been in the second half of the twentieth century. Of course this statement is difficult to substantiate, since much depends on the definition of 'town', the occupational structure of the urban population, and so on.

Pre-industrial urbanism

Max Weber has argued that the only time and place where the true urban community has existed was in medieval Europe. Such a community, he asserted, should be based primarily on trade and commerce and generally had the following features:
1 fortification;

2 a market;
3 a court of its own and at least partially autonomous law;
4 a related form of association;
5 at least partial autonomy with burghers taking part in the election of urban administrators.

Essentially, then, the city emerges out of feudal society as a distinct and largely autonomous community. 'City air makes one free' was an adage in medieval Germany and in England: a serf who escaped to town and lived unchallenged within its walls for a year and a day could claim to be regarded as a free man. Generally, urban dwellers belonged to professional groups such as crafts or guilds, localised within the urban areas. Within the ward or street districts, urbanites had specific responsibilities for maintaining the peace: social control was maintained both formally and informally.

Weber suggested that such ideas of 'urban citizenry' or 'urban community' appear to be lacking in Far Eastern cities. Cities acting specifically as cities, as a particular kind of communal action, are the product of a distinctively European tradition. Urban freehold, property and trade were the bases of the class of burghers, independent of the feudal lords. 'During the period of maximum autonomy', Weber remarks, 'the cities displayed an exceptional variety of forms and trends.' Some cities pursued imperialistic foreign policies, having their own soldiers and even controlling overseas colonies. Some large cities in Italy and Germany achieved an international political importance. This was not the pattern in England where cities were always limited in their power, largely because, although the king did grant charters allowing a degree of autonomy to cities from the twelfth century, crucial military and political power was centralised in a way which made English feudalism quite a separate sort of system from that which developed in France or Germany.

Perhaps the best way to see pre-industrial cities is by analysing the sources and distribution of power. Firstly, there was the power struggle between the individual cities and the central authority. Secondly, there was a struggle between cities for various privileges and trade monopolies, particularly the struggle between the overwhelmingly dominant London and other cities.

And, finally, there were struggles within the city for political power, trade and craft privilege, the rights of minorities, and so on. The city as a sociological fact could not exist without its power.

Professor Sjoberg has described other characteristics which, he claims, are typically found in an ideal type of pre-industrial city. In terms of spatial arrangements, he mentions the segregation of minority ethnic groups, the congestion within the walls, the dominance of the central area and low functional differentiation. He sees a direct link between the technological base of a society and the localisation of particular crafts and merchant activities in segregated quarters or streets. Such pre-industrial cities are essentially centres for the elite: only there can they communicate and maintain their common interests. 'The more potent the elite, the grander the city.' The elite has power rationalised through religion and maintained through the control of education and government. Sjoberg argues that the merchants are excluded from the elite, despite the city being dependent on commerce. 'Business men, or merchants, fall into the lower class or outcaste group.' The social structure is said to be rigid and there is very little social mobility. The economic structure is based on the guilds. Most economic transactions are concluded after long haggling. There is little specialisation of function in craft industrial production, although there is a good deal of product specialisation.

Sjoberg also discusses marriage and the family, the political structure, the religious structure, and so on. His book has given rise to a great deal of controversy and he has been severely criticised by historians and sociologists, largely for generalising about *the* pre-industrial city which, he claims, has common characteristics remaining much the same 'over fifty-five centuries' and between different cultures. Such broad generalisations are sharply at variance with the work of Weber, who stressed the variation and distinctiveness of pre-industrial cities largely as reflections of the distribution of power in society. There may, indeed, be certain similarities between contemporary 'pre-industrial' cities, but to argue that they are essentially the same type in that they are all 'pre-industrial' is hardly defensible. Not only does Sjoberg, in Wrigley's phrase, do violence to history (Wrigley 1978), but he also does violence to sociology. Nevertheless, his work is widely read and quoted.

It is in this context that the following, more detailed, accounts of York and London should be seen. We are still a very long way from a sociological theory of pre-industrial urbanism and urban-isation in Britain. Quite apart from the intrinsic interest of such a study, it is important to understand that cities are not simply products of the last 200 years. The industrial revolution may have helped to form an urban society, but the distinctiveness of urban life was, in certain respects, more marked in the centuries which preceded it.

It is also important to stress the variations in pre-industrial cities. As we shall see, there was an important distinction between London and the other provincial cities, but there was a hierarchy below this level, ranging from the larger provincial cities through the county towns to the smaller market towns, which were often barely distinguished from villages. Cities also varied according to their economic function and their regional hinterland, and their prosperity depended importantly on these factors. This leads to the final variation – the major changes over time. Pre-industrial cities were not static, nor did they grow at a steady rate. In most periods, there were cities which were prospering and growing, and others which stagnated and declined. This might be because of physical changes – coastal towns might suffer from erosions or silting, as Dunwich and Great Yarmouth did in the fourteenth century. One town might grow at the expense of another, as Reading did at the expense of Wallingford. A group of towns depending on a particular industry might suffer from increasing difficulties if that industry went into a decline. Finally, epidemics could have disastrous effects, reducing a town's population by a third or more at a single blow. However great the political auton-omy of towns, they were highly vulnerable to economic and phys-ical processes outside their control.

Medieval York: the emergence of urban autonomy

Medieval York provides an example of the working of the dis-tinctive urban institutions of a community of traders and craftsmen (Miller 1961). Until the year 1212, the sheriff of Yorkshire had to provide revenues for the king and these were probably derived from tolls and other charges on the trading activities of the citizens, a simple tax on domestic property and revenue from the urban court. Furthermore, the king imposed extra levies: between 1156 and 1206 there were sixteen of these, yielding some £3,500, which would be a considerable burden on the citizens. In the later part of the twelfth century, the citizens were granted the right to found an association on the coast and in Normandy. Nevertheless, it is interesting that some basic civic liberties are thought to have been laid down without the warrant of a charter, so that even as early as the beginning of the twelfth century such rights of citizenship may have been established for some time.

In the early years of the thirteenth century the citizens of York were given the collective responsibility for the management of urban finances, thus emancipating them from the power of the sheriff. Later in the same century citizens acquired further legal rights – for example, they could be convicted only by a jury of fellow citizens, except when the city as a whole was charged. Legal, financial and commercial autonomy meant that the citizens had effectively pre-empted the authority of the sheriff and were, by the mid-thirteenth century, directly responsible to the central government. Even so, it is important to emphasise that, unlike some continental cities, York was not truly independent: all her privileges were dependent upon the king's grace.

During the thirteenth century York gradually acquired its distinct civic constitution. It had a mayor from about 1212 and other officers such as coroners, chamberlains (or financial officers) and a beadle were appointed soon afterwards. Citizens were expected to play an active part in self government: the butchers' guild was responsible for the city gaol at night and parishes had formal responsibilities connected with the apprehension of escaped prisoners. A small ruling elite provided the mayors during this period and it was common for the same man to be re-elected five or six times and then for his son to follow afterwards. A recurring problem during the century was the inability of the citizens to raise sufficient revenue to meet the demands of the national Exchequer: this may have been due partly to the fact that 'prominent citizens' had certain tax privileges which were not available to the 'lesser folk'. This was a source of social tension which in some towns produced serious urban riots. The urban elite of thirteenth-century York appeared to have little sense of *noblesse oblige*: as the city's historian Edward Miller puts it: 'The civic officers had failed to act on royal writs, took bribes, levied excessive charges on bakers, and hanged out of hand a man accused of theft when he made certain accusations against some of the *majores* of the city.'

An extremely important right held by the citizens of York was the ability to own, inherit and sell private property. Urban tenements are likely to have changed hands frequently and a body of tenurial custom emerged constituting a *lex civitatis* different in many important respects from the common law of England. The evolution of urban customs into what were in effect civic by-laws was an important element in the development of a distinctive urban consciousness.

A further source of tension in the urban situation developed between the ecclesiastical elite, concerned to defend its distinctive rights and privileges, and the lay urban government. The mayor and citizens were disinclined to respect exemptions from various tolls and taxes at a time of financial difficulties. Running battles between the ecclesiastical and civic elites continued through the century.

Social and geographic mobility and rural–urban linkages

The growth of York was based on a high level of immigration, which continued to the end of the Middle Ages. Migrants from the surrounding villages added to the Anglo-Scandinavian core of the city and helped to counterbalance the high urban mortality. A wide range of places throughout northern England provided the source of these migrants who maintained links with their rural kinship networks. Cities provided a crucial avenue of social mobility from the constraints of rural feudal society but it was probably necessary for those with few resources to have a patron who could help to ease the transition to urban-based networks and urban institutions.

It is extremely difficult to say anything precise about the social processes in a medieval city. There are, however, lists of the men admitted to the freedom of the city. During Edward I's reign, for

TABLE 1.1 *City of York: admissions to freedom 1272–1509*

Craft groups	Per cent of known occupations				
	1272–1306	1307–1349	1350–1399	1400–1449	1450–1509
Textile	7	14	28	21	21
Provision	29	23	11	14	17
Mercantile	10	16	16	15	11
Leather	30	22	15	12	13
Building	2	3	6	8	7
Metal	17	13	11	11	10
Miscellaneous	5	9	13	19	21
% freemen whose occupation is not stated	40	23	12	11	9
Total freemen	767	2,540	4,838	4,870	4,086
Av. freemen/yr	26	59	97	97	68

Source: Miller 1961.

example, it seems that some 30 percent of these were craftsmen in the leather trade and those engaged in the provision trades comprised 29 percent. The remaining freemen fell into the following categories: metal crafts 17 percent; commerce and shipping 10 percent; textile crafts, mainly tailors, 7 percent; miscellaneous occupations 5 percent; and building crafts, 2 percent. It does appear that this community of craftsmen, working for a restricted market, had within it broad extremes of wealth. In a tax return of 1204, out of a total of £375, thirty-two men contributed £212 between them: of these ten paid £10 or more, four from £5–10, three from £1–5 and fifteen under £1. Men with considerable wealth appear to be very few indeed: these were the merchants who provided the city's elite. Some of these merchants acquired extensive property – both in the city and in the rural areas; some provided loans to country landowners. All this helped to ensure permanent links between urban and rural areas and helps to explain the stability of York's ruling elite in the twelfth and thirteenth centuries.

The emergence of a community power structure

We are told that 'it was a tight little group which ruled the city at this time' and we can be more sure of this since it is the wills and other records of the very rich people that remain for the historian to correlate. The records of the poor are scant. The city's liberties continued to be extended in the fourteenth century but the power of the ruling elite remained concentrated – in the half-century ending in 1372 only fifteen names appear in the list of mayors. By the end of the century candidates for the mayoral election were restricted to aldermen. Royal intervention in the later fifteenth century attempted to let the crafts have greater power in the election of aldermen. This threat to the oligarchical power of the mayorality was resisted: yet the property owners' power could not be maintained. Out of eighty-eight mayors between 1399 and 1509 one was a glazier, one a spicer, one a pewterer, and one a vintner; there were three drapers, four grocers and goldsmiths, and five dyers; but sixty-eight were merchants or mercers. To quote Professor Miller again: 'So far as the mayorality is a measure of it, the government of late medieval York was not so much an aldermanic as a mercantile oligarchy. It was the merchant who had stepped into the place of the property-owning patrician of earlier times.' Furthermore:

A small, close knit oligarchy filled civic offices and seats in the council chamber. More than that, these men were bound by ties of occupation. As early as 1378–9 the aldermen appear to have been drawn exclusively, and the councillors preponderantly, from the class of wealthy traders. Of the 1420 council, five belonged to manufacturing crafts, but two were drapers and twenty-two merchants. York was ruled not merely by an oligarchy, but by a mercantile oligarchy.

This does little to support Sjoberg's notion of the relationship between the merchant and the elite mentioned above.

Craft organisation

It is difficult to know how many guilds there were in York: various lists give between fifty and eighty names of crafts but industrial activities were finely graded and there was a good deal of trespassing on others' province. There were also various amalgamations and combinations. The ordinances of the guilds were drawn up by the masters of the craft but received their force from enforcement by the city authorities, and hence guild officers were responsible to both the city council and their craft. This responsibility for industrial organisation on the part of the city meant that civic authorities arbitrated in disputes between guilds – indeed the city had the power to disband guilds if they were completely recalcitrant.

The most important guild officer was the searcher, who was appointed by his predecessor and was answerable to the city authorities for the standards of workmanship in their craft. Searchers summoned guild meetings, managed its finances, 'searched' the articles made by guild members, approved the technical skill of new masters and of 'strangers' coming to the city, authorised the taking on of apprentices, and often inspected the quality of 'foreign' goods coming into the city. The carpenters employed four searchers and also an employment officer for their craft. Often other men were appointed to help the searchers assess penalties. Other guild regulations included the prohibition of night work, work done outside a master's house, and the employment of more than one apprentice by a master. Officers of the guild controlled entry, ensured that 'foreigns' had appropriate testimonials and took the entrance fee of 20s. All these rules supported jointly by city and guild were to maintain quality control in the interests of local consumer or export merchant.

Apprentices normally had to serve for seven years and the industrial unit was generally limited to the master, his wife and one apprentice, perhaps supplemented by journeymen or servants. In 1401 the searchers of the spurriers' guild allotted immigrant labour to the master whose need was greatest due to lack, death, or illness of a servant. Later in the century immigrant workers had attempted to organise collective action to negotiate better wage rates. 'The city authorities intervened and forbade servants to form their own organisations or to persuade other servants to leave their master or the city. On the other hand a master was to pay a workman for whom temporarily he had no employment, and piece rates were amended generally in an upward direction.' By no means all apprentices became freemen: 'In 1482–83, out of sixty-five apprentices who completed their terms, only thirty-eight became freemen forthwith. The rest paid a lower fee to pursue their callings in the city, presumably as journeymen, though some of them became freemen in later years.' Yet the activities of guilds were not limited to economic affairs: they also operated as charities, giving alms and associating themselves with religious activities, particularly the famous Corpus Christi plays.

The urban social structure

Inequalities of wealth in medieval York have already been mentioned: a further tax return of 1327 shows that only one man had goods worth more than £26 and only fifty-five (7 percent) at £5 or more. On the other hand 61 percent were assessed at between £1 and £4 and 32 percent had goods worth less than £1. Clearly very few men were wealthy and of these only a fifth were merchants, the rest being craftsmen of various sorts. Whilst there was clearly a hard core of urban poor the poll tax returns of 1377 show that a third of all taxpayers had servants. However, whereas only a few craftsmen had a servant, merchants generally had five or six and one had eight.

The social significance of the metropolis

The social composition of medieval London

In medieval England London was a unique city in size and organisation, resembling more the great continental cities rather than the larger provincial centres, such as York or Bristol, compared

TABLE 1.2   *London population 1501–2*

Citizens			Estimates of total persons
Merchants	1,200	with wives, children and apprentices	6,300
Other citizens in company livery	1,200	with wives, children and apprentices	6–7,000
		aliens of superior rank	500
Small masters and workers	2,000	with wives, single women, children and apprentices	7,000
		foreigns, small masters and workers with families including suburban population	10,000
		aliens, small masters and workers with families including suburban population	2,500

Source: Thrupp 1948, p. 51.

with which it was at least three times as large. In 1501–2 Thrupp has calculated that there were some 3,400 citizens out of a population of some 30 or 40,000. Only those who had sworn loyalty to the city government and had undertaken to bear their share of taxation and public duty could style themselves as citizens or free men and claim the various privileges that were guaranteed to the community by royal charter. Those who were unenfranchised were 'outsiders' whether born in or outside London and were termed 'foreigns': these were often the poor – the porters, water carriers and casual labourers, some of whom came in from the suburbs and surrounding country. In 1463 the city authorities attempted to keep foreign shopkeepers segregated. Those who were born overseas were called 'aliens'.

Social and geographical mobility and rural–urban linkages

London's links with the rest of the country were wide ranging: from perhaps the twelfth, and certainly the thirteenth, century onwards citizens were buying country property, not simply as an investment but also as a pleasant place to live. The subsidy roll of 1436 shows that citizens' country properties were scattered in almost every English county except the far north. These properties satisfied the merchant's love of business, pleasure and display but the country was also considered a healthier place to be, particularly in times of urban epidemics. 'I undystonde they dy sor in London', wrote one merchant urging his brother to come out to his place in Essex. Building new manor houses in the country was as popular as the improvement and renovation of existing property in need of attention. Apparently many of the merchants and other rich men of London had been brought up in the country either being entrusted as babies to village nurses or spending long holidays in the country. These childhood memories may have helped to retain an affection for rural life amongst the merchant class, many of whom set themselves up in country houses near London. Even when elected mayor at the end of the fifteenth century, John Warde tried to continue living in Hertfordshire and only the threat of a £500 fine brought him and his family into town. Retirement in the country was popular – mainly in the home counties.

Both merchants and members of lesser companies must have maintained kinship links with provincial towns and rural areas: evidence from London wills shows that they were anxious to leave generous legacies to country kin. Sometimes executors were instructed to distribute money among poor relations or to the poor of the neighbourhood in their 'country'.

Movement from the merchant class into the landed gentry was often achieved by buying a country property: older families might consider the merchant who maintained his London connections as simply a *nouveau riche*, but if he had been a sheriff, alderman or, better still, mayor then he could certainly gain status. Marrying his daughter into the local gentry was one of the surest ways of a family acquiring superior status in the second generation.

Not only did the merchants take London into the provinces, London also drew on the rest of the country and indeed, without a steady stream of immigration, the population would have dwindled. The merchant class could not have maintained itself without recruitment from outside and this would apply with even more force to the other citizens and the unenfranchised. From early in the fourteenth century, therefore, London was recruiting apprentices from the whole country. Thrupp shows that the main area of recruitment shifted from the home counties through the Midlands to the north as the century progressed. Some indication of this is shown by an analysis of the wills of rich merchants who left money to people in the area in which they were born (Table 1.3).

TABLE 1.3   *Wills of rich merchants*

Region of birth	Merchants dying 1450–1515 (N 139)
	%
Home Counties	24
East	27
Midlands	28
North	10
West	9

Source: Thrupp 1948, p. 210.

Thrupp suggests that apprentices were recruited from diverse social origins and many merchants came from the trading and artisan elements in the villages and small towns. Others had been trained in larger towns and were able to buy themselves the freedom of the city. At the end of the fifteenth century perhaps between a third and a half of all immigrant apprentices, who were being accepted in the main London companies, came from families already engaged in industry and trade, mostly in the smaller towns and villages.

The social and demographic impact of London on the provinces in the sixteenth and seventeenth centuries

London as a capital city grew to be the largest city in Europe by the end of the seventeenth century. Quite apart from its importance as the home of the Royal Court and the Courts of Justice it was also a centre of conspicuous consumption for the nation's gentry. With its many private schools and the Inns of Court it developed so rapidly as an educational centre that the historian F. J. Fisher estimated that by the reign of Charles I 'the majority of the country's gentry' were spending the most impressionable years of their lives there. And even when they were settled on their estate London was still of outstanding importance as a centre of litigation, as a money market, as the centre of the political world and, of course, as the source of a bride with a large dowry (Fisher 1948).

As it became the custom of the gentry to winter in London, luxury trades expanded and King James complained of 'Those swarms of gentry who, through the instigation of their wives and to new-model and fashion their daughters (who if they were unmarried marred their reputations, and if married lost them) did neglect their country hospitality, and cumber the city, a general nuisance to the kingdom' (quoted in Fisher 1948).

Given the rapid population growth of London – that is the addition of some 275,000 between 1650 and 1750 – then an average of 8,000 immigrants a year over the period would be needed to cover the shortfall of births over deaths. In a recent paper E. A. Wrigley (1978) has made some very interesting calculations. He assumes that since it is the young and unmarried who are most likely to migrate and since this category would represent a birth population half as large again and since, finally, the average surplus of births over deaths in provincial England was 5 per thousand per annum, then London's growth was absorbing the natural increase of a population of some $2\frac{1}{2}$ million! This is even more remarkable when one remembers that the population of England, excluding London, was only about 5 million at this time and that in many areas of the West and North there was little natural increase or indeed there was a decrease in these areas.

In the light of these calculations and assumptions Wrigley claims that one-sixth, or an even higher fraction, of the total adult population of England 'at some stage of their lives had direct experience of life in the great city'.

The comparison of London and York has revealed the important qualitative differences between London and the provinces. It is also important to understand the changes going on in English cities in the three centuries before the Industrial Revolution; that is, between the beginning of the sixteenth century and the end of the eighteenth. This period saw a marked loss of political and cultural autonomy of the cities, but eventually a marked gain in economic vitality even before the start of the Industrial Revolution.

The varied economic fortunes of different cities have already been noted, but some historians have argued that there was a general process of urban decline in the late medieval period which saw a loss of population and economic activity, particularly in the larger provincial centres. Charles Phythian-Adams (1978), for example, discusses the case of Coventry, where 25 percent of the city's housing was vacant in 1523, and where population is estimated to have fallen from about 10,000 in 1440, to about 8,500 in 1500 and under 5,000 in 1563. The economic problems of the city were also revealed in a growth of urban poverty which led to moves to register and control beggars, and in an increase in the incidence of riots – Coventry was said to have been out of control for two weeks in 1525. Coventry was probably the worst case, but there does appear to have been something approaching an urban crisis in the early part of the sixteenth century.

Phythian-Adams argues that this crisis reflects an underlying transformation in the role of cities. He argues that there was a process leading to economic decline of the cities relative to the rural areas. There was an increasing resistance to guild restrictions on manufacture and also to the considerable costs of urban residence, associated with guild and church ceremonies. Manufacturing was tending to grow in rural areas outside the cities, beyond the reach of these costs and constraints. Phythian-Adams documents the considerable extent of public ceremony in Coventry in another article (1972) and argues that it played an important role in bringing together the church, the guilds and the institutions of the city, and promoting communal solidarity over sectional interests. It was a major element in the political and cultural autonomy of the city. The structure of public ceremony largely collapsed in the first half of the sixteenth century under pressure of economic decline and the Reformation. Over the next 150 years landed society increased its political and cultural role at the expense of the cities. Many cities, of which Bath is the most notable, were effectively colonised as meeting places and centres of consumption for the landed gentry. This could lead to economic revival, with substantial rebuilding and the growth of many craft industries.

However, in this period the towns had an even more important economic role – their central place in the development of capitalism. The development of capitalism involved two related processes: the increasing organisation of the production of goods for the needs of the market rather than the immediate consumption of the producers, and the social organisation of production on the basis of a division between capital and wage labour, freed from the bonds of serfdom and the protection of the guilds. As the nodal points of trade and exchange, with their concentrations of merchant capital and skilled workers, the towns played a crucial role in the early concentration of capital for production for the market. The early stages were relatively slow. They did not see the growth of factory industry, nor even a very substantial increase in the population of the towns. Capitalist production often took place in rural areas, particularly in the textile industry. Moreover, economic growth depended on a surplus of both food and people from the rural areas. The important point is that the economic reorganisation of the country increasingly depended on the town. Conversely, the town was ceasing to be, if it ever was, an autonomous economic entity, and was becoming ever more closely tied into the structures and processes of the whole society.

2

THE EMERGENCE OF INDUSTRIAL URBANISM IN BRITAIN

We have seen that there was an uneven pattern of urban growth in the centuries before 1800. In the eighteenth century urban growth became more general and cities grew in prosperity. However, it is in the nineteenth century that the pace of change increased radically and that a number of very large industrial cities appeared. The extent of this quantitative change is not in doubt, but sociologists are interested in whether these changes have brought real qualitative changes in social relationships.

In 1801, 9.73 percent of the population of England and Wales lived in London and only a further 7.21 percent lived in towns of 20,000 people or more. But by the middle of the century the urban population of Britain was greater than the rural and, indeed, since 1911 four-fifths of the population have lived in areas defined as urban. The period from the 1840s to the 1870s showed the most rapid rates of urbanisation, although places such as Manchester, which doubled its size in the first thirty years of the nineteenth century, were ahead of the national pattern.

However, the aggregate figures of urban growth in the nineteenth century give a very oversimplified view, and may be positively misleading if one is concerned with what happened in particular regions or localities. For example, there were enormous variations in the rates of growth of county populations. Between 1801 and 1911 the population of Lancashire grew by 607 percent, while that of Oxfordshire grew by 70 percent. Villages and small towns often lost population, not just because of changes in agriculture but also because the cheap factory production of many commodities in daily use, combined with efficient transport through the railway system, displaced many rural craftsmen.

The growth of the industrial towns and cities was largely due to high rates of natural increase of the population in the rural areas and county towns immediately surrounding the booming industrial centres. For example, Anderson shows in a study of Preston that 70 percent of migrants to Preston were born within thirty miles. There were differences in the distances which skilled and unskilled workers moved. For example, 67 percent of the unskilled labourers working in the naval dockyard at Sheerness in Kent were born in that county, compared with 32 percent of the shipwrights and skilled metal workers. Indeed, there would seem to have been something approaching a national labour market for the skilled workers. The shipwrights came from other naval towns, such as Devonport and Pembroke, and from ports such as Sunderland and Great Yarmouth. Sizeable migration flows linked these places. In general, however, there was relatively little long distance movement from north to south – the differences in population growth rates being caused by considerable emigration from the south to North America and substantial inward movements to parts of the north from Scotland and more particularly Ireland, and 'little Irelands' appeared in many northern industrial towns.

Thus population growth was very uneven, but so also was economic growth. The same processes of capital accumulation, improved transport, technological innovation and increased industrial production in response to growing home and overseas demand lay behind urbanisation, but the way these processes affected individual cities was very different. Preston, Manchester and Brighton were all creations of the nineteenth century Industrial Revolution. The first was a centre of textile manufacture in large factories, the second manufactured a wider range of goods and operated as a commercial centre for the north-west, with a growing army of cotton merchants and clerks, while the third developed as a tourist resort where the higher incomes which industrialisation brought to some of the population could be spent.

There were also marked differences in the rates of population growth, and places such as Middlesborough and Barrow-in-Furness grew up as boom towns almost overnight. In 1864 Barrow had a population of 8,176, a trebling of the population in three years. Such breakneck urbanisation meant that houses were thrown up quickly and cheaply; local government barely existed, if at all, and in many places there was no provision for any services. An article in *The Times* of 8 February 1871 on the problems of administering the census illustrates the situation very graphically:

There are many towns containing long lines of cottaged streets, formed by the gradual coalescence of buildings erected by several small proprietors; and in such streets it's not uncommon for each proprietor to give his little road a distinctive name, and to number the houses it contains from one upwards, without the smallest regard to the numbers in the vicinity. In Nottingham there was formerly a long street which was said to repeat its numbers up to three no less than 30 times . . . A resident there would give his address as 'The fifth number 3 on the right hand side as you go up', for such names as 'Matilda Place' or 'Eliza Cottages' had long been swept away.

Urbanism and class-consciousness in nineteenth-century towns

Historical urban sociology has been rather slow to develop in this country and so we have had to make do with Engels' description of the working class in Manchester or Booth's description of London at the end of the nineteenth century and the work of non-sociologically informed historians. Hence we know very little about the process of urbanisation, seen not merely as an aggregation of population within certain administrative areas, but rather, qualitatively, as the restructuring of social relationships within an urban – industrial milieu. The most dramatic sociological consequence of the various technological and other changes, which we term the Industrial Revolution, was the crystallisation of a class society.

Economic and social historians have debated amongst themselves how much *real* poverty there was in nineteenth century towns, how bad the health and housing may have been and other such problems mostly defined by the Reports and Royal Commissions of contemporary social reformers. The dramatic emergence of an urban – industrial society created new social conditions as well as new physical conditions. How did these newly created and expanding towns react as social entities? There has been a welcome development of an interest among historians in community history and local social systems at previous periods of time; but just as no modern industrial sociologist would expect to find the same response under different technological systems and work situations, so also should the urban sociologist expect different urban systems to invoke different responses.

Research by John Foster, a Cambridge historian, provides an example of the kind of urban history of most interest to urban sociologists. He undertook careful historical analysis of what he terms 'the class dimension' in Oldham, Northampton and South Shields in the early nineteenth century. He was concerned with the immediate context that moulded a man's social behaviour: whom he married, where he lived, how he worked and what he hoped for. In a phrase, he was looking at the differential life chances in different industrial – urban situations. Foster analysed the various social categories of his town in terms of occupation, industry, birthplace, family structure and so on, and also analysed marriage certificates in order to assess how open or closed specific status groups were. Finally, he analysed the available documentary evidence in order to test his hypotheses about class-consciousness in particular. The results are some extremely penetrating case studies of the class reactions to emerging industrial – urbanism. What follows is a direct paraphrase of his work.

Oldham

In Oldham by 1851 two-thirds of the borough's labour force of 40,000 were employed in the coal-mining, cotton and engineering industries. These industries were highly capitalised, with control concentrated with a small number of families; for example, 80 percent of the engineering workers were employed by three big firms. There was very little chance of social mobility and there had not been much change during the early period of capitalisation: all except one of the early cotton firms were founded by small landowners switching over from out-work manufacturing. These yeomen manufacturers had been building up their capital from the mid-eighteenth century.

Thus at mid-century there were 12,000 worker families selling their labour to seventy capitalist families. The capitalist families were very rich – annual incomes ranged between £3,000 and £10,000 – and most owned estates in other parts of the country. Incomes of worker *families* ranged from £50 to £100 – insufficient to keep any but the top 15 percent of highly-paid craft workers *permanently* out of primary poverty. One worker child in five died before its first birthday. One female mill worker in every seven died while in the age group 25–34 (mostly of TB). One miner in every five could expect to be killed during a normal working life. Up to 1850 mill hours were never much below 12 a day, six days a week. Nor could the system guarantee even this minimal existence. There were the regular periods of mass unemployment – sending the proportion of families in primary poverty at *any one time* well over 40 percent. This was the class situation with which people had to come to terms. For the first 50 years of the century their reaction was to fight it (Foster 1968, pp. 284–5).

For a period of fifty years from the 1790s through to the 1840s a small group of people worked consistently to overthrow the system. By controlling the police for a period, together with certain other local powers, the working class maintained a measure of control. They were able to do this by threatening to boycott local shopkeepers unless they voted appropriately at local elections. The essential precondition of class formation, argues Foster, following Marx, is that people *think* it is possible to change things. He brings forward a number of contemporary statements and accounts which support his contention that the workers were analysing the local situation in terms of class. For example, the following is part of a resolution passed in 1838 at a mass meeting of Oldham workers:

. . . that labour is the source of all property; without a surplus of labour has been performed and property produced no accumulation of property can take place . . . that it is an indisputable fact that the various classes of capitalists have the whole power of making and administering the laws, which is almost uniformly done for their own benefit . . . that the time has now come when Englishmen must learn to act instead of talk (quoted in Foster 1968, p. 289).

Foster argues that this degree of working-class solidarity required considerable organisation and mobilisation both to keep control of local government and to prevent class splitting up into status groups as a means of accommodating social inequality. Partly there was simply coercion by the workers of the workers to maintain this solidarity. However, Foster also produces evidence to show that marriages between labourers and highly paid craftsmen were far more frequent than in South Shields, where there was no class conflict and where there was a highly developed hierarchy of occupational neighbourhoods. For more than a generation the social structure in Oldham, below the seventy capitalist families, remained remarkably open.

The local bourgeoisie was similarly remarkably united. Foster was able to analyse friendship clusterings, that is to say groups of people who went to each other's weddings and funerals and acted as mutual executors. Those with substantial capital were closely tied together by kinship and marriage into a closeknit network. Within this network were two main clusterings. The 'traditional' bourgeoisie lived in quasi-rural situations on land they had occupied for centuries, growing richer as the men who worked for them grew poorer. The other cluster Foster terms 'cosmopolitan', many of these also had traditional peasant backgrounds but now employed labour in the crowded central core of the town. They did not develop social relationships locally as much as with others in Manchester and the County aristocracy.

Between the capitalists and the workers was a very small 'middle class' of tradesmen, small employers and masters. Such a group had a limited stake in the system and shared a common belief that they were hard done by. The small man, despised and intimidated, fighting grimly for economic survival, watched the town's bourgeoisie taking its annual 10 percent while their own neighbours appeared one by one in the bankruptcy court. The tradesmen (town centre food wholesalers, drapers, printers, corn millers, etc.) were mainly concerned with keeping their working capital intact (rarely above £5,000) and maintaining their essential links with outside supplies and customers. The greatest recurrent threat to a family's working capital (and its trading connections) was a series of bad marriages. The group therefore kept exclusively together, insulating its members from undesirable contacts. The little masters (commission spinners, waste dealers, millwright, jobbing builders and so on) had little use for working capital or outside links. They worked for local markets and needed only skill in their trade and an ability to organise small-scale production. They tended to merge socially if not politically with the working class.

This, then, is the class society in Oldham in the early nineteenth century as analysed by Foster. How does this compare with other nineteenth century towns with different patterns of industrial–urbanism?

Northampton

At the beginning of the nineteenth century Northampton mainly served as a supply centre for the country's landed society or as an agricultural market. In the 1820s and 1830s people moved in to the developing shoe industry from the surrounding countryside so that by 1851, with a population of 26,000, almost half the labour force was employed in the shoe industry. Production, requiring no fixed capital, was organised on garret sweat-shop lines, and London merchants mostly supplied the credit and made the profits. Northampton had none of the tight completeness of Oldham in its community structure. Tory hoteliers and lawyers, whig-dissenter corn and wool dealers and radical garret masters split elite politics in three ways. Even though primary poverty was, if anything, more severe than in Oldham, nevertheless class formation was slight. 'Working-class' politics remained those of an occupational subgroup – not of labour as a whole. The old hierarchical status system held up. The workers moved from the village to the town but the old county aristocracy were not far away. The shopmen, coachwrights, furniture makers, and brewery workers remained Anglican and deferential. For the shoemakers the unemployment and poverty in the countryside, which they had just left, contrasted unfavourably with their immediate situation and perhaps distracted attention from it.

South Shields

The situation in South Shields was different again. Half the labour force was organised round shifting coal down to London. There were 200 ships distributed among 150 owners: small men, tradesmen, provisioners, shipbuilders, and so on investing their savings. This activity provided a common overlap for almost every South Shields trade – keelmen, dockers, provisioners, and sailmakers – and this was reinforced by interlocking insurance and broking clubs which formed a sort of unofficial town senate. Because of all this, admission to the town's elite (such as it was) was comparatively easy.

A further difference in South Shields was the absence of work for women and children, which augmented family incomes in other towns. Hence the family income differential between, say, shipwrights and labourers stood out more sharply and the labour-force remained socially fragmented. In this situation, with no resident bourgeoisie, there was little scope for class formation.

Discussion of the three towns

In the early nineteenth century, and possibly in modern societies which have not fully developed the media of mass communication, people's idea of their society came mostly from their immediate community. While both South Shields and Northampton each had by the middle of the century less than a dozen men who would leave fortunes of over £25,000, Oldham had seventy and the fortunes of many of these were considerable. Furthermore, social mobility with the elite was much more restricted in Oldham. Engels had noted the importance of a 'resident bourgeoisie' in accounting for the different class reactions in Birmingham and Manchester. Much depends, as Weber also noted, on the 'transparency of the connection between the causes and the consequences of the class situation'. The problems which a historian faces in recreating such a situation are daunting and hence the importance of Foster's work.

The more typical reaction of the working class in later nineteenth-century provincial England was to withdraw from a confrontation with the total social success system by holding as their reference groups smaller sub-cultures with their own, more limited, versions of success. Thus, in order to avoid uncomfortable comparisons, members of each sub-group have to be *socially* similar with roughly the same job, income and way of life. The group's identity is then fixed in terms of the existing order, each group having its own 'pride' and its own 'respect'. The South Shields sailors had their 'loyal standard'; late nineteenth-century Oldham clerks their paper-collar 'gentility'. Each group defined itself negatively, particularly against other groups with less good life chances.

Thus for a status group structure to crystallise into a class struggle much will depend on the local urban – industrial situation. More recent work on the inter-industry propensity to strike has brought together convincing evidence of the more strike-prone nature of isolated bodies of manual workers such as miners, deep-sea fishermen or dockers. Political sociologists have also noted more radical voting behaviour in more isolated communities in which manual workers are encapsulated from the dominant norms and values of the wider society. Foster also believes that where there are employment opportunities for women and children, semiskilled and unskilled manual workers were able to bring up the level of their family incomes, thus helping to overcome something of the sub-cultural distinctions. However, even if working-class sub-cultures can be coalesced, there still remains the problem of whether the sub-culture will remain basically 'respectful', or deferential, or whether it will demand a confrontation with ruling-class authority. It is here that the local urban – industrial system is crucial.

Social control in nineteenth-century towns

The threat of radicalism and social disorder was not restricted to Oldham, and in many places it led to a concern about means of social control. In the early part of the century many industrialists preferred to have their workpeople close to the works, not only to ensure punctuality but also as a means of social control. Thomas Chalmers was urging in the 1820s in a three-volume work on *The Christian and Civic Economy of Large Towns* that cities should be split into smaller localities in order to prevent the people 'forming into a combined array of hostile feeling and prejudice'. Industrialists were alert to the dangers of 'the unmanageable mass' and saw many advantages of an employment monopoly in an industrial village. Many industrial villages in Lancashire remained self-sufficient, independent communities and such villages also existed within borough boundaries. These 'urban' villages may well have had as strong a sense of separateness as those industrial villages in more rural settings. Where the employer plays the benevolent-squire role, contributing to schools, bathhouses and the Mechanics Institute, then, as the urban historian J. D. Marshall puts it, 'the idiocy of village life might be rejuvenated and even strengthened in its industrial context' (Marshall 1968, p. 226). Of course, whether this is sociologically accurate is largely a matter of conjecture.

The problems of social control were much more acute in the

large cities, and the middle class fear of social disorder perhaps reached its peak in London in the last third of the nineteenth century. This has been analysed by Gareth Stedman Jones (1971) in his study of the casual labour market and the middle class response to it, *Outcast London*.

The casual labour market in late nineteenth-century London

As in the pre-industrial period, London's social and economic structure was quite unlike that of other British cities. London's economy had four main supports: its role as a capital city, which concentrated government institutions and the legal system; its role as a financial centre and as a major port; and its role as a centre of consumption for the wealthy. Thus the working class in London were mainly employed around the port or in providing goods and services for immediate consumption. Both these sources of activity fluctuated substantially through the year, with the variation in trade and the London 'season'. As a result, in a great many trades employment was extremely irregular and, because the labour supply tended to meet the peaks in demand, there was considerable under-employment during the rest of the year. The same factors also meant that most firms were very small, and thus that there was practically no organised or unionised body of workers.

Exacerbating these endemic characteristics, towards the end of the century London's industry began to suffer increasing competition from the provinces. Some industries, of which shipbuilding was the most notable, collapsed completely in the face of competition from areas with lower wage rates. In other industries there was a move towards factory production which was more efficient than small-scale artisan production, but which was almost invariably outside London. For example, Northampton and Leicester developed as shoemaking centres at the expense of London. The effect of this was to depress the standard of living of those who continued to try to work in London, unless they were working strictly for the luxury markets. Those thrown out of their trades by these processes joined the increasingly intense competition for unskilled work, in the docks for example.

These characteristics of London's economy also meant that London's upper and middle class were very distinctive. There was no class of large manufacturers, and the social elite of London was made up of those whose incomes derived from rent, banking and commerce, and also of a large professional class. As a result, class relations in London were not dominated by conflict between capital and labour, or even by the form of accommodation between them which paternalistic employers often produced in the northern factory towns. In London, the distance between the classes was much greater, and the middle class response was one of fear of the threat of social disorder which poverty promised to bring. There grew up an ideology which saw the slums, particularly those of the East End, as the haunt of criminal and revolutionary classes who threatened to break out at any moment, and whose influence contaminated the whole of the working class of London. Such views were reinforced by the outbreaks of rioting which spread from the east and south London into the West End in 1866 and again more seriously in 1886 and 1887.

The middle-class response

The response to this perceived threat took three main forms. In the first place it promoted a considerable body of social investigations into the problems of poverty and bad housing, notably Charles Booth's *Life and Labour of the People of London*, published between 1889 and 1903, and revelations of the depths of poverty, such as Andrew Mearns' *The Bitter Cry of Outcast London*, published in 1883. The shock which these writings produced led to the second response, a philanthropic concern with the problems, and a very considerable level of private charity. This was also linked to early developments in social work, such as the university settlements, set up by graduates in the slums. However, these responses were linked to the third response, the call for greater social control.

Indiscriminate charity was criticised and it was argued that it should be limited and controlled, so as to prevent the growth of dependence and pauperism. The working class should be 'moralised' into habits of thrift. Towards the end of the century it began to be argued that it was necessary to separate the more respectable and regular sections of the working class in order to protect them from the influence of the casual workers and the 'criminal classes' who were barely distinguished. To this end radical members of the Liberal Party argued that the state should help workers to exercise thrift, through unemployment insurance schemes. The corollary of this was that more authoritarian methods should be used to control the remainder. Among the methods suggested were the setting up of work colonies outside London, overseas emigration, and even the sterilisation of the unfit. Though none of these solutions were ever implemented, the contradictory attitudes lying behind them were an important contribution to the development of state intervention to deal with urban problems. The same features may be seen in the early stages of urban redevelopment and the provision of public housing. Road improvement schemes often had the explicit aim of destroying concentrations of poverty and crime in the slums. The first public housing scheme similarly often destroyed slum housing and replaced it with housing at rents which made it only available to the more regular workers. The effect was to create new slums as those who had been displaced looked for cheap housing elsewhere. We shall see in later chapters that twentieth century state intervention to deal with urban problems could be equally contradictory and Stedman Jones's study is valuable for showing the sorts of broader processes of class conflict and industrial change which could lie behind it.

Towards a sociology of urbanisation in Britain

We have seen that the mere concentration of population within administrative areas, designated as urban, says little about the qualitative changes involved. Indeed, many large cities were simply agglomerations of industrial villages. Furthermore, the response to urbanisation may vary widely. Between generalisation so broad as to be meaningless and the minutiae of the parish or ward's social history, it is necessary to provide some kind of framework into which detailed local information may be fitted. We shall try to provide such a framework based on the important processes in this final section.

The migration process

1. The social structure of the area of emigration. It is important to know whether the urban migrants came from *closed* villages, where at least half the acreage is owned by the squire himself in residence, or by an absentee landlord, or from *open* villages in which there are a significant proportion of peasants and freeholders. One would expect towns which largely recruited their populations mainly from one or the other type would differ markedly, peasants or freeholders being more independent-minded and more ready to seek radical solutions to the problems the urban situation thrust upon them.

2. *The social structure of the receiving area.* We have already seen something of the variety as between Oldham, Northampton and South Shields. It is important to know whether migrants worked for one or a few employers in paternalist industrial villages, or whether they moved into large, speculatively-built urban estates. They may move into an established, even if rapidly growing, town with at least some facilities and social and political organisation, or they may move into a completely new town. Depending on the different occupational and industrial structures of the towns, so the response of the migrants to the urbanisation process will be different.

3. *The nature of the links between areas of emigration and immigration.* Much depends on the actual physical distance the migrants have travelled. Where they have moved only a short distance they will be able to maintain kinship linkages with parents and siblings, who may have remained behind in the villages. Similarly, where people from a similar area move into a nearby town they are able to provide each other with social and economic support. This may take place as much with, say, Irish immigrants coming from a similar part of Ireland and settling together in a quarter of an English town, or for local migrants from nearby villages. The social controls and cultural patterns of the previous milieu may be maintained, transformed or developed in the new situation.

4. *The age/sex balance of the migrating population.* Sometimes a town may grow gradually so that its age structure may be reasonably balanced. In other cases all the migrants may be young men and women in their twenties and thirties with young chil-

dren, who of course will all grow old together, leading to a bulge moving through the age pyramid. In towns where there is a high demand for male employment with very little for women and children it may be that the immigrant population has a very unbalanced sex structure. The temporary preponderance of men may on the one hand lead to vice, drunkenness and prostitution; alternatively, the lack of alternative employment may lead to poverty and overcrowding as people are obliged to share dwellings to minimise the cost of rent. However, this point should not be over stressed. The strong demand for female domestic servants served not only to balance the sex-ratio but also, in some cases, to unbalance in the opposite direction so that men were heavily outnumbered for a time.

Encapsulation or assimilation

1. Industrial villages. If countrymen from the surrounding area move in, bringing their pigs to keep in their backyards, and are surrounded by friends and kin from their area of origin, then they may stay encapsulated within the urban system for a hundred years or more. There need be no sharp break in primary or secondary group ties; houses may be owned and retained in the family; jobs may be found for their children when they are old enough and later they may marry and settle down in their own or one of the neighbouring urban – industrial villages. Despite the census evidence there would not be any great change in their way of living as a result of urbanisation. Some of the more rural customs will decline, to be sure, but the break will not be traumatic and vestiges of the earlier culture will linger on for many years. Stella Davies' book *North Country Bred* (1963) is well worth reading in this context. However, here again it is worth remembering that none of this would apply for the more mobile workers. We must be very cautious about how much we can generalise from the particular.

2. Assimilation by association. Social historians emphasise the plethora of voluntary associations during the early period of urbanisation in Britain. Some of these were basic instrumental activities; for example, the forms of forced savings such as the Benefit or Friendly societies, being collective responses to individual crises and problems. These voluntary organisations were a direct response to urbanism and were, as the Hammonds put it, 'the defences of the poor', in their book on *The Town Labourer* (1966).

The man who has no share in the government of his parish or mill needs some scope for his political capacities; the man who spends his life 'making the twenty-fourth part of a pin' needs some sphere for his imagination; the man whose only provision against accident or illness or the loss of his livelihood is the reluctant succour of the poor law, needs some protection against fortune; the man who lives under the unbridled power of employer and magistrate needs some protection against that power, some pledge of help and friendship in the hour of struggle and tribulation. These necessaries of his larger life the English workman sought during the Industrial Revolution in organisations that he created and developed under the fierce discouragement of his rulers.

Documentation of these voluntary associations is available in many of the standard social histories.

3. From the urban village to the urban system. The voluntary association very often served as a bridge between the individual's local system of industrial village or segregated occupation or craft to the wider urban society. However, it was only when men saw the situation in larger terms, and became aware of their class position in the wider society, that they may be said to be truly urbanised. Hence a large proportion of the population in the nineteenth century was urbanised in the demographic sense but had not yet moved into the urban system to be urbanised in the sociological sense. They were in the city but not of it. This is an important distinction and hence the relevance of Foster's work on class formation discussed above. If Northampton shoe-makers were still operating with rural reference groups – that is if they were comparing their lot favourably with friends and kin in the villages they had left – then their meaningful social world was not yet the town. The switching of reference groups and the restructuring of normative behaviour to the large-scale society should be the essential focus of a sociological approach to urbanisation.

When we reach the late Victorian and Edwardian periods a new range of sources on life in cities becomes available. There is a growing body of work in oral history, which has tapped the memories of old people of the period before the First World War.

The most notable project in this field, covering the whole country, was undertaken by Paul Thompson at the University of Essex. Some of the results were published in his book, *The Edwardians* (1975). More detailed studies have also been undertaken, such as Jerry White's *Rothschild Buildings* (1980), which looked at life in a London East End tenement block. Together, these and other works show the diversity of urban life in the period when urbanisation was complete in a demographic sense, but, more important, as Standish Meacham argues in his book, *A Life Apart* (1977), they show the separation of social classes within cities. The Edwardian period is in many ways the classic period of urban working class culture. The important feature of this culture is the extent to which it was insulated from outside influences. The cities were made up of a mosaic of little worlds, between the railway tracks, with their own norms of behaviour and social structures. One such area is vividly portrayed by Robert Roberts in his account of his childhood in Salford, *The Classic Slum* (1973). The extreme localism of working class culture was already beginning to be broken down in this period by industrial change, the suburban growth of cities and the growth of working class politics and the First World War also played an important role in this process. Nevertheless, the patterns of segregation in British cities have persisted, and in the next chapter we look at their significance.

Urbanisation and the family

The impact of urbanisation on the family may be considered in two ways: in the first place, the nature of the work carried out by different family members changed and, secondly, the growth of large towns may itself have had some impact. The theme of the family and work will be considered further in Chapter 7, but the importance of the change that industrialisation and urbanisation brought about needs to be emphasised. Generally, in the pre-industrial period the family was the working unit and the home was also the place of work. There was not a simple division between the role of wage earner responsible for bringing resources into the household and a housewife responsible for preparing these resources for consumption and maintaining the household. All these tasks were performed by all members of the household. This was true in both agricultural communities and in many artisan trades. Tilly and Scott (1978), in their study of women's work, argue that in aggregate the change which the Industrial Revolution brought about was not so much in the type of work done by women, though for a minority work in large factories was qualitatively new, but rather in the social relations which surrounded it. The change was that many more women were working outside the home and were working for wages. The same was true for men, but the implication of the change was an alteration in the economic relations between the sexes. In towns without a significant amount of work for women, the effect of the separation of home and work was to reinforce a division between men as wage earners and women as housewives. However, in many towns in the industrial north there were large numbers of women working in the textile factories. Thus the wages of wives and daughters could be an important element in the family income. There were indeed cases where a wife's income could be larger and more regular than her husband's, and the primary support of the household. In many cities work was more easily obtained by children than by adults. These factors may have altered the balance of power within the family. They increased the ability of children to leave their parents' home, and the fact that there was no property in the form of a farm to be inherited reduced their incentive to remain. Conversely, parents had considerably more incentive to keep children at home. Unfortunately, we have very little direct information about the quality of family relations in nineteenth-century cities. For most of the century we have had to rely on contemporary accounts of outside observers.

In 1845, Frederick Engels published a vigorous attack on the urban-industrial system: *The Condition of the Working Class in England*. Leaving aside the polemics, however understandable in the contemporary situation, Engels's work is still one of the most perceptive accounts of urban social conditions and the section on 'The Great Towns' is based on personal fieldwork as well as documentary and statistical analysis, particularly on the city of Manchester. He argues, with most other Victorian social reformers, that the appalling physical conditions in the great industrial cities were having severe effects on the health, physique and moral and social relationships of the working population. Historians do not all accept the typicality or extent of the conditions described in contemporary reports of the early nineteenth century but certainly parts of such cities as Leeds, Liverpool, Glasgow, and Manchester were as foul as the most lurid descriptions portray. It was in this context that Engels wrote:

Thus the social order makes family life almost impossible for the worker. In a comfortless, filthy house, hardly good enough for mere nightly shelter, ill-furnished, often neither rain-tight nor warm, a foul atmosphere filling rooms overcrowded with human beings no domestic comfort is possible. The husband works the whole day through, perhaps the wife also and the elder children, all in different places; they meet night and morning only, all under perpetual temptation to drink; what family life is possible under such conditions?

Clearly one needs to know how general such conditions were. In Oldham two related families at different stages in their life cycle would combine to form one household. A husband and wife with young children would live with their parents, being supported by them and by unmarried siblings while their own children were under the age of eight or nine, and then later on when their children went out to work they would repay their parents by then supporting them. This huddling together of the impoverished working class varied between towns and over time. Overcrowding would be matched by a large number of empty houses, which would be inhabited or not depending on local economic fluctuations. The proportion of households in Oldham in 1851 containing three generations, and sometimes also siblings and related families of the same generation, was 21 percent. In Northampton the figure was 14 percent and South Shields 11 percent.

Certainly in some parts of some cities primary group relationships, particularly the family, were less stable, and symptoms of social disorganisation such as drunkenness and vice are well-documented. Often such conditions were very short-lived, associated with the rapid immigration of young unmarried men, presenting the same kinds of problems as appear today in African mining towns.

Any attempt to make qualitative judgements about the nature of family life at different historical periods and under different economic conditions is an extremely hazardous exercise. However, as Peter Laslett (1965) emphasises: 'It remains the case that there slept together under each roof in 1600 only the nuclear family, with the addition of servants where necessary. Therefore in that vital respect one's ancestors were not different from ourselves. They were the same.' Laslett's book is essential reading for demythologising the past. The 'normal' state of affairs in pre-industrial England was for the parents and children of the nuclear family to live separately, with extra-familial kin living in the vicinity. For a time, in some cities, a proportion – probably a minority – of families shared the same living arrangements with extra-familial kin. This so-called 'extended' family household was not any kind of typical pattern: paradoxically, urban-industrialism had the effect of *over*emphasising family relationships as a form of defence and security. This is shown by Michael Anderson's (1971) very careful study of Preston: From a study of census and other primary data he argued that kin relations were the most important means of dealing with what he calls 'critical life situations'. Thus someone migrating to Preston would stay on their first arrival with kin who had moved there earlier, and they would also fall back on the support of kin in crises such as unemployment. Hence to talk today about a 'decline' in the 'extended' family is a curious sort of nonsense. For a certain section of the population over a limited period of time, linkages with extra-familial kin were overstressed. As the system settled down the dominance of the nuclear family reasserted itself.

Hence Engels' statement about the family is most misleading. There is an implicit assumption that housing conditions in rural areas were necessarily better and there is a lot of evidence to the contrary. Further, he implies that the quality of a relationship depends on length of face-to-face contact. If that were the case, we should be equally concerned about present-day long-distance commuters to the city of London who are away from the house for eleven or twelve hours, and whose children are at boarding school. The problems of the working class under the conditions of early urban – industrialism were acute and in many respects similar to those in the rapidly growing cities of Latin America, Asia, and Africa today. Like present-day urbanising peasants, their response to this situation varied, but the most remarkable thing, surely, is the strength of the family to adjust and adapt to the demands put upon it.

3

PATTERNS OF URBAN LIFE?

A number of observers, from Engels in 1844 and Booth in 1889, had recognised that urban life was distinctively patterned. Specific districts of cities acquired their own distinctive characteristics and social style, and people increasingly recognised that they lived not so much in the cities such as London, Manchester or Birmingham, but more in areas, such as Bermondsey, Ordsall or Saltley (for the working class), or Hampstead, Victoria Park or Edgbaston (for the middle class). The emergence of these distinctive social worlds which had been described with varying degrees of sophistication by the early sociographers emerged in more dramatic style in the rapidly expanding American cities which received migrants not only from their own rural areas, but also from many culturally distinct rural areas in Europe. In an attempt to come to terms with both the cultural diversity and the developing urban life of Chicago in the 1920s, the first major school of urban sociology was born.

Ecology and the Chicago School of urban sociology

Many of the terms used to describe the socio-spatial structure of urban areas were first used by urban sociologists at the University of Chicago in the interwar period (Park *et al*. 1925). Cities were described as having a characteristic structure and pattern of growth said to have general application. E. W. Burgess, for example, described Chicago in terms of a series of concentric zones having distinctive social and physical characteristics, which, he claimed, might be generally true for all cities (see Fig. 3.1). Other research workers emphasised the wedge-like

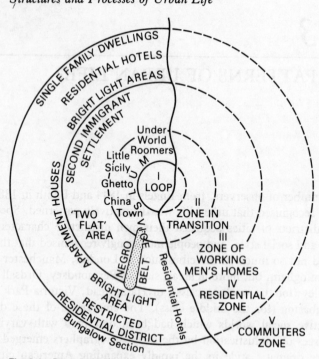

Fig. 3.1 Burgess's diagram of city ecology

character of urban growth or the multiple nuclei structure, with each nucleus having a distinctive function or social character.

The Chicago School of urban sociology also investigated the so-called 'natural areas' of cities which together formed 'a mosaic of little worlds which touch but do not inter-penetrate', in R. E. Park's phrase. This segregation was seen as a physical fact re-inforcing social distance, with each area having its own sub-cultural values and contributing to the 'natural' life of the city. The processes which produced these segregated or 'natural' areas were partly social and partly sub-social. Park sought to understand the sifting and sorting mechanisms which 'select' appropriate indi-viduals to live in appropriate areas: ultimately, he said, it is *com-petition* – the struggle for space – which allocates people to their position in society and their position in space. The division of labour involves 'competitive co-operation' and, borrowing heavily from ecology, Park described society in terms of symbiotic relationships (Park 1952).

Those in the most 'dominant' position controlled the most valuable part of the city – the central business district (CBD). Next to this is the zone in transition, which, at the time when the Chicago sociologists were doing their studies, was a colourful and varied area of slums, bohemia, immigrant ghettoes, rented rooms, and so on. Clearly they were concerned with a particular city at a particular period of time with a given technology, so that their understanding of the processes of growth and change was not always very clear. The zone of transition presumably had different social characteristics in the past and would have different social characteristics in the future. Not all receive successive waves of immigrants who 'invade' certain areas of cities leading to 'dominance' and ultimately 'succession' of the new element. According to this ecological approach, people are gripped by a kind of economic determinism over which they have little or no control. Contemporary urban sociologists accept the importance of social ecology as a valuable descriptive tool, but reject the sub-social ecological framework on which much of the early work was based.

Spatial structure in historical perspective

Before considering some recent analyses of British cities, it is instructive to consider British urban spatial structure in perspective. The peculiar characteristics of urbanism in this country need to be seen in historical context and most of our towns and cities retain many spatial characteristics relating to an earlier period of growth. Unlike American cities, European cities have grown and developed from medieval origins and this has important implications for the socio-economic pattern today. Hence, although British towns have their CBDs, they also have their cathedrals, castles and physical remains of other medieval institutions. Such features are symbols of other value systems which may or may not reinforce the system based on profits and rents. Generally, of course, the lay or ecclesiastical elite introduced differential rents, charging more for property and frontages which were better protected or more accessible to customers. Nevertheless, economic competition did not produce the kind of ecological segregation which is more characteristic of modern cities. There was some segregation by trade or craft, so that towns developed distinctive functional areas, but rich and poor were not so sharply separated in a physical sense, partly because medieval cities were smaller than their modern counterparts.

This lack of segregation before the seventeenth century may be partly explained by the relatively slow rate of population growth and the difficulties of extending the existing built-up areas. The town's political privileges related to a limited area which it was difficult for it to extend. Hence, urban densities increased at the expense of social segregation. Small cottages were squeezed between more substantial houses and rich merchants, unable to get land at the periphery, even if they wanted it, were obliged to build high on existing central city plots. Medieval suburbs were as socially mixed and as physically heterogeneous as the centres. Admittedly, certain sites attracted higher values – for example, merchants clustered in the fashionable Radcliffe area of Bristol in order to get river frontages to their gardens – but other merchants in that city would rather live in towers built upon the city walls than have a long journey to work. Privacy did not seem to be highly valued.

Contrast between provincial and metropolitan spatial structures

One of the most distinctive features of English urbanism is the contrast between London and the provincial cities. The metropolis developed a distinctive social and spatial structure not matched by other English towns. As early as the sixteenth century, historians noted the polarisation between the industrial and impoverished area east of the city and the wealthy area stretching westwards to Westminster and the Court. In 1662, Petty remarked on the 'pallace of the greatest men' in the west as those escaping from the 'fumes, steams and stinks of the whole easterly pyle' left the old great houses of the City which then became halls for companies or were turned into tenements. This polarisation became even more acute towards the end of the seventeenth century when new, planned, residential development in the west, coupled with the rapid expansion of population, drew the rich and poor further apart. The implications of this spatial segregation for social policy were seen clearly by Colquhoun, a police magistrate for the Tower Hamlets, who described the situation in 1797:

The lower classes [in the eastern parishes] are compelled to contribute largely to the fund for supporting the poor from the daily pittance which arises from labour . . . while in almost every other part of the metropolis, as the rich form a considerable proportion of the inhabitants . . . the burden does not attach. And thus it happens that in Spitalfields and Mile End New Town from five shillings in the pound are paid . . . and after all extremely inadequate to the wants of the poor, while St. George's Hanover Square and St. Marylebone paying only two shillings to two and sixpence in the pound, and the poor are abundantly fed, while the labouring poor in that part of the town are eased of a heavy burden. (quoted in George 1965, p. 332 n)

This overall polarisation, which emerged between the sixteenth century and the eighteenth, was superimposed on a poly-nuclear pattern more typical of the pre-industrial city. London was divided into Park's 'mosaic of little worlds', partly because of difficulties of communication, partly because of rigid lines of demarcation between trades and occupations and partly because of the local government structure. However, Mrs George, the historian of *London Life in the Eighteenth Century*, claims that by the beginning of her period the distinctiveness of the small localities had been lessened.

Segregation as a function of population concentration and increase, and social mobility

The enormous expansion of urban populations in the nineteenth century created new and distinctive patterns of urbanism. The concentration of the labour force in factories led to the rapid development of estates of cheap working men's cottages built as closely as possible to the centres of employment. The rise of the new middle class, based on the growth of manufacturing industry, produced new housing demands quite out of scale with the previous situation in provincial towns. The horse-drawn tram and later the railways helped to carry the middle class away from the working class. As industrialism and economic growth produced

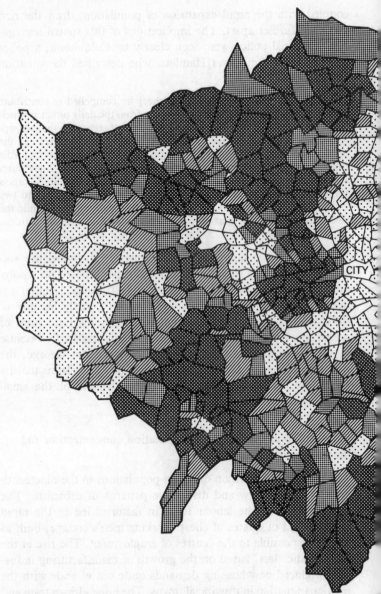

Fig. 3.2   Distribution of Professional and Managerial Workers in London: 19
(Source: T. Shepherd, J. Westaway and T. Lee 1974, p.61)

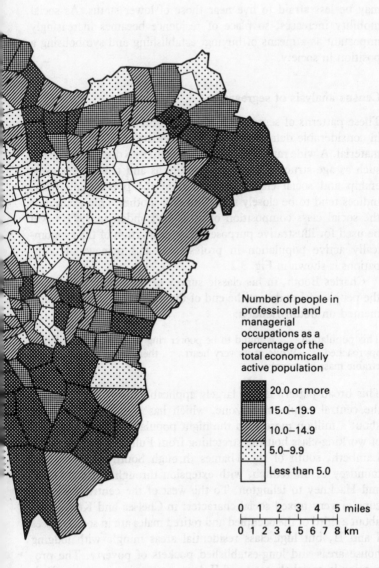

Number of people in
professional and
managerial
occupations as a
percentage of the
total economically
active population

20.0 or more

15.0–19.9

10.0–14.9

5.0–9.9

Less than 5.0

0 1 2 3 4 5 miles

0 1 2 3 4 5 6 7 8 km

its new and expanding class structure so people increasingly sought to make clear, by where they lived, their position in the social structure. People who are sure of their position in society may be less afraid to live near those of lower status. As social mobility increases, so place of residence becames increasingly important as a means of buying, establishing and symbolising a position in society.

Census analysis of segregation

These patterns of segregation in many cities have been analysed in considerable detail through the systematic analysis of Census material. A wide range of indices can be used to distinguish areas, such as age structure, housing conditions and tenure, car ownership and social class composition of the population. These indices tend to be closely related to one another. One example – the social class composition of areas in London in 1971 – will be used for illustrative purposes. The proportion of the economically active population in professional and managerial occupations is shown in Fig. 3.2.

Charles Booth, in his classic survey of the labour and life of the people of London at the end of the nineteenth century, commented on South London:

This population . . . is found to be poorer ring by ring as the centre is approached . . . While at its very heart . . . there exists a very impenetrable mass of poverty.

This broad pattern is still largely applicable today. Surrounding the central employment zone, which has a day population of about a million more than the night population, is a broad belt of working-class housing stretching from Fulham, Battersea and Lambeth, south of the Thames through Southwark and Bermondsey to Shoreditch, with extension through Bethnal Green and Hackney to Islington. To the west of the centre there is a zone of very mixed social character; in Chelsea and Kensington about a third of the occupied and retired males are in social classes I and II, but high-class residential areas mingle with lodging house areas and long-established pockets of poverty. The proportion in social classes I and II drops on moving north into Paddington, but increases to between a third and a half of the total population in Hampstead.

The main middle-class areas in the south, from Orpington to Surbiton, and into the Surrey suburbs beyond the Greater London area, are separated by the working-class East End and the industrial areas of West London – Acton, Hammersmith and Willesden – from the north-west middle-class suburbs stretching from Wembley and Harrow through Hendon to Barnet and Potters Bar. A further industrial belt stretching up the Lee Valley separates the north-west middle-class suburbs from the north-east middle-class suburbs of Woodford, Chingford and Chigwell.

Certainly there is something of a concentric pattern in the social class map of Greater London, despite the extension of industrial belts to the west and up the Lee Valley. However, new public housing built over the last thirty years has enabled or obliged more working-class people to live further out. Conversely, over the past twenty years there has been a substantial movement of people in professional and managerial occupations into the centre of London in a process known as 'gentrification'. This involved the modernisation or conversion into flats of previously working-class housing in areas such as Camden and Islington. Ironically, when this housing was first built in the nineteenth century it was largely for middle-class occupations.

Distinct social worlds based upon social class or cultural diversity can co-exist reasonably easily even to the extreme that Zorbaugh documented in his study *The Gold Coast and the Slum* (1929) – the very rich and the very poor along Chicago's lake side. Such co-existence is not always possible when conflict based on race or religion deepens to an extent that one's life depends on where one lives and how one sets about making the ordinary journeys of everyday life. The last twenty years have seen an increased scholarly focus on such conflicts, stimulated by the collapse of social order in Ulster and potential violent conflict based on ethnic differences in the inner areas of British cities. We now turn to discuss some of these studies.

Segregation and conflict in Belfast

The study of Belfast carried out at the Geography Department of Queens University by F. W. Boal, M. A. Poole and their colleagues looked at residential segregation and residential mobility in the Belfast Urban Area (that is the County Borough plus the surrounding built up area) in the period from 1969 to 1972 – the first four years of the present 'troubles'. However, they also traced back the links between segregation and conflict to the middle of the last century. A commission of inquiry into the riots of 1857 reported:

Since the commencement of the riots . . . the districts have become exclusive and by regular systematised movements on the sides, the few Catholic inhabitants of the Sandy Row district have been obliged to leave it, and the few Protestant inhabitants of the Pound district have also been obliged to leave that locality.

Similarly, a report on the riots of 1886 said:

The extremity to which party and religious feeling has grown in Belfast is shown strikingly by the fact that the people of the artisan and labouring class, disregarding the ordinary considerations of convenience, dwell to a large extent in separate quarters, each of which is almost entirely given up to persons of one particular faith, and the boundaries of which are sharply defined.

The Belfast study analysed segregation at the level of the street and distinguished between three types of areas, which they labelled 'Catholic City' 'Mixed City' and 'Protestant City'. 'Catholic City, included those streets where the proportion Catholic lay between 91 and 100 percent (in practice, most such streets were 100 percent Catholic). 'Protestant City' was composed of streets that were 91 to 100 percent Protestant (again, mainly 100 percent). 'Mixed City' contained streets in which the proportion in each group lay between 10 and 90 percent. In 1972 it was found that 70 percent of the population of the Belfast Urban Area lived in either 'Catholic City' or 'Protestant City' – that is, in the highly segregated areas – and that the proportion thus segregated was about the same for both groups. Thus, 68 per cent of Catholics lived in 'Catholic City' and 71 percent of Protestants in 'Protestant City', and about 30 percent of both groups in 'Mixed City'.

The three 'Cities' were not continuous areas, but there were some concentrations within the city as a whole. 'Catholic City' (shown in Fig. 3.3) was concentrated in the city centre and in a

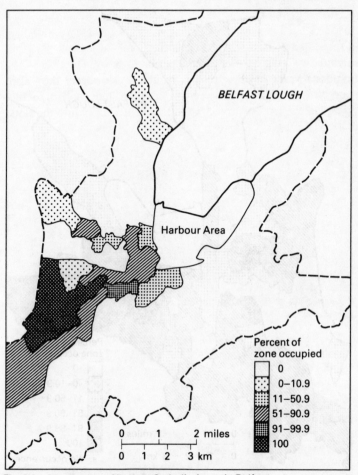

Fig. 3.3 Distribution of Roman Catholic Areas in Belfast
(Source: F. W. Boal, R. C. Murray and M. A. Poole, 1976)

radial sector to the south-west, following the Falls Road. Because of its greater overall size, 'Protestant City' (shown in Fig. 3.4) was more dispersed, but it dominated East Belfast and also areas in the south and north-west. 'Mixed City' was also dispersed, but there was some concentration along a north-south axis.

One of the most striking findings of the study was the extent to which segregation had increased in the four years from 1969

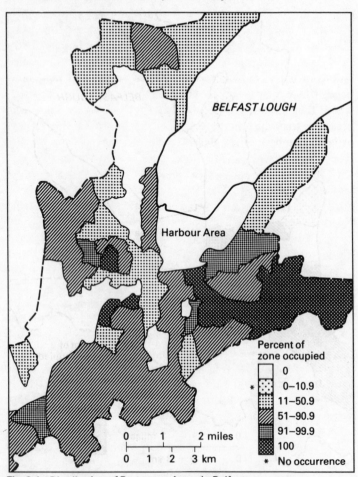

Fig. 3.4 Distribution of Protestant Areas in Belfast
(Source: F. W. Boal, R. C. Murray and M. A. Poole, 1976)

to 1972. Using data only for the County Borough, it was shown that the proportion of the population living in 'Catholic City' and 'Protestant City' increased from 67 to 77 percent, either as a result of people moving into segregated streets, or of streets changing character as the minority moved out. This change followed directly from the 'troubles'. Their sample survey showed that over 20 percent of those moving in this period stated the 'troubles' as the reason for the move – with reasons ranging from the disturbed state of the immediate area to direct intimidation of the household. Households moved from four types of areas: firstly, from 'front-line' areas which became intolerable due to manifestations of overt conflict; secondly, from streets and neighbourhoods where their group formed a minority; thirdly, from streets where their group had been a majority, but where there were pressures from the other group, since that group was the recipient of large numbers of immigrants who had moved from the first two types of areas. Finally, households moved within their own 'city' to try to get away from areas which were perceived to be particularly disturbed. The housing market and the public housing system often broke down in these conditions, and housing allocation was undertaken by para-military groups.

Boal *et al.* (1976) argue that residential segregation performs important functions in a situation of underlying conflict between groups. It reduces contact between the groups and thus lessens the chance of conflict in day-to-day life, and also aids the preservation of the cultural integrity of each group. Boal, in an earlier study of a small area on the dividing line between Catholic and Protestant areas between the Shankill and Falls Roads shows that not only is residence segregated, but also activity patterns. He shows that significant numbers walk further to shops or to bus stops than they would have to if they were prepared to enter the area perceived to belong to the other group (Boal 1974). Segregation becomes much more important when conflict is overt. It provides a source of physical security and a basis on which defensive and aggressive organisation can be built. This may become more important in a situation of overt conflict as the level of centrally provided services declines. Thus, in May 1974 during the Ulster Workers' Strike:

. . . the whole of Northern Ireland faced a situation where electric power was being progressively run down, causing a complete industrial stoppage and where again the agencies of government were effectively paralysed. In such a situation, the urban community groups in Belfast came into their own, and it was not an exaggeration to talk in terms of community self-management. In concrete terms this meant organising the passage of food and drink, the provision of meals or cooking facilities, seeking alternative energy supplies, the creation of community transport systems and caring for the old, the sick and disabled. And, whereas in

1971 local communities still relied a good deal on the services of outside agencies, by 1974 they had developed the self-confidence and the structure to take over local administration. (Boal *et al.* 1976)

It is notable that it was in some of the more mixed middle-class areas that local community organisation did not emerge.

Of course, segregation also has a number of negative consequences. In particular, it is often argued that segregation serves to perpetuate the conflict by intensifying the cultural identity of each group and setting up clear dividing lines between them. Segregation of residence and activities may also increase inequalities, by trapping the groups in sub-sections of the housing and labour markets. For example, it is argued that higher levels of Catholic unemployment are a consequence of the location of most workplaces in Protestant areas, combined with the unwillingness of many Catholics to enter these areas.

Nevertheless, Boal *et al.* (1976) argue that policies of desegregation would not be a solution in Belfast:

We have stressed that in an endemic conflict situation, such as that which exists in Belfast, residential segregation becomes a critical mechanism for group survival. It could be argued, however, that group survival perpetuates the conflicts, but if one takes this position one can only propose assimilation of one group by the other, or total victory by one group or the other in conflict resolving (terminating?) processes.

The study of Belfast shows that national conflicts which are not themselves based on conflicts over space can take on a strong spatial dimension within the city. Increased spatial segregation was a consequence of conflict, and territory took on considerable symbolic significance. The study shows the way that specific social processes, such as the Irish conflict, rather than universal ecological processes can lie behind the spatial structuring of the city.

Ethnic minorities in British cities

Another ethnic group division which has been studied in terms of patterns of segregation is that of the position of coloured immigrants in British cities. Many studies have found such groups to be highly concentrated in inner city areas, though the degree of segregation has not been as high as that found in Belfast between Catholics and Protestants. There are no areas exclusively occupied by one non-white ethnic group. Sociologists have been concerned with how the concentrations have arisen and with their consequences for race relations.

The major study in this area has been that by Rex and Moore in the Sparkbrook area of Birmingham, carried out in the mid-1960s and published in 1967. This concerned above all the processes in the housing market which trapped immigrants in the zone of transition.

The emergence of sub-cultural styles

Three main groups became segregated from each other during the early growth of the city. First, the upper-middle class or 'captains of industry' lived in substantial family houses. Economically and socially independent, and secure in their possession of capital and property, they were able to develop their own distinctive style of community living relatively close to the centre of the city. Secondly, those who were employed by the upper-middle class, as so many rent-paying hands, were housed in rows of little cottages and for them common deprivation helped to create common solidarity. A common culture emerged in which extra-familial kin, pubs and chapels, the trade unions and the friendly societies were of great importance.

The final category, which began to emerge towards the end of the nineteenth century, was socially and economically between the two main categories; this category, shopkeepers, clerks and other lower-middle class people, aspired to the style of life of the upper-middle class and went as close towards it as their more limited means would allow.

Such is a somewhat oversimplified model of the social structure which produced the spatial structure of the city of Birmingham eighty years ago. It was based on the industrial and employment structure of the time and reflected contemporary ideologies and the distribution of power. This structure then became fossilised in bricks and mortar so that the houses still stand in what is now an inner zone which, when the houses were built, was the edge of the city.

The urban game of leapfrog

With time, the large family houses ceased to be so convenient or so fashionable. The increase in population, the development of the motor car, buses and trams, all served to push the upper-middle class to large detached houses, gaining quietness and privacy and large secluded gardens, further out from the city centre. The lower-middle class may have had to leap further out to their semi-detached houses, with gardens back and front, and were dependent on the availability of cheap land and their ability to borrow capital. The working class were also able to join in this suburban game by using the power they had gained in local government to build cheaper replicas of white-collar housing, also on the cheaper land at the periphery. Thus a new public suburbia paralleled the private suburbia. The demand for cheap land and space, coupled with the inevitable decay of older properties, creates a pattern of central decline and peripheral expansion, which continues until the core is renewed.

The urban socio-cultural system

The leapfrogging suburban development implies a general acceptance of the middle-class style of life as a common aspiration for all sections of the population. It is because of these common values and common objectives that there is conflict over housing. Those who are left behind in the centre of the city may still accept the urban value system, which implies that they are at the back of a queue to move to the most desired style of life in the suburbs. Hence, those who live in the city's inner ring are more likely to see their stay there as *transitional*. Rex and Moore (1967) saw this urban central status value system as crucial in understanding the problems of this zone of transition:

Any attempt to segregate the inhabitants of this area permanently is bound to involve conflict. The long-term destiny of a city which frustrates the desire to improve their status by segregationalist policies is some sort of urban riot. (p. 9)

Rex and Moore argued that in Birmingham overt and covert discrimination operated in public and private housing sectors to trap immigrants in the zone of transition. In particular, the allocation procedures for council housing, such as the priority given to those who had lived in Birmingham longest, prevented coloured immigrants gaining access to the more desirable estates. As a result, newcomers without large amounts of capital had to shelter in the converted middle-class houses of the inner rings of the city. The immigrant who borrowed from relatives and friends could, with the help of a bank or money-lender, acquire sufficient capital on a short-term basis for him to buy a lodging house and repay the loan if he got a high income from rents. Thus, there was a need for houses in which no one else had a long-term interest, with sufficient rooms to ensure a high rent income. Those who rented the rooms would be those who valued the anonymity and impersonal market relationship with the landlord, and those who simply could not find alternative accommodation. Hence such districts included immigrants, 'deviants' of one sort and another, people with irregular forms of family life, and so on. Characterised by over-crowding, high rents, lack of privacy and no choice in neighbours, such a housing situation produces a very diverse housing class which 'lacks the capacity and perhaps the desire to organise itself as an interest group. The discharged prisoner, the deserted wife, the coloured immigrant and the prostitute have little in common except their housing conditions' (Rex and Moore 1967, p. 38). This section of the population has to be housed and 'A pariah group of landlords is needed who will do an essential job and take the blame for doing it,' (pp. 40–41).

The landlord was not in a strong position. He might have been obliged to pay a very high deposit – perhaps up to 50 per cent of the cost of the house – and be obliged to repay the rent at a high rate of interest. Indeed, he might repay both a bank and building society and his friends or relatives at the same time. The houses produce very little capital when sold: those built in the 1880s and 1890s probably have ninety-nine year leases which would expire in ten or fifteen years' time. Inevitably, multi-occupation leads to neglect, as tenants have no stake in maintaining the value of the property. Furthermore, Pakistani landlords might feel obliged to provide accommodation for their kinsmen, either rent-free or at a nominal charge of £1 a week. This cuts his total income, since there was a limit which he could hope to squeeze from his other tenants. These may include more than his fair share of deviants or those with large families, who give the fabric of the property hard use. Thus the debt-burdened landlord, surrounded by difficult tenants, was unlikely to have much money with which to maintain, far less improve, the property. Moreover, the perception of existing inhabitants that the immigrants are responsible for these results will exacerbate race relations in the area.

Rex and Moore argue from their study of Birmingham that these processes are part of a wider class struggle over the use of housing, which is distinct from class conflicts derived from the labour market, which can be seen as the central process of the city as a social unit. This argument will be considered in the next chapter. However, it is notable that other studies of race relations in inner city areas show very different situations from those found in Birmingham.

Davies and Taylor (1970), for example, found that in Newcastle Asian immigrants had little desire to enter the public housing sector. They regarded the purchase and sub-letting of houses as a means of capital accumulation and preferred to own their homes to paying rent to a landlord. They found that in Rye Hill, an area of about 600 houses, while Indians and Pakistanis comprised 6 per cent of Rye Hill's population, 18 per cent of the houses were owned by these groups. Several Asians owned more than one house, and 45 per cent of the houses owned by Asians had an absentee landlord. Davies and Taylor argue from these figures that Asian landlordism in Newcastle cannot simply be seen as a means for Asians to solve their own housing problems. They argue: 'the general picture, then, within which there are very considerable variations, is one of an acquisitive and self-reliant attitude to property, and of a similar positive evaluation of independence and enterprise in careers'.

Robin Ward carried out a study of race relations and housing in Moss Side, in Manchester, and contrasts this case with that of Birmingham and a number of other studies (Ward 1978). He argues that in two important respects local features of the areas which immigrants entered had a bearing on the process of residential succession and the extent of racial conflict. The first of these local features was the condition and status of the housing in the area. Ward argued that where, as in Birmingham, the arrival of the immigrants coincided with or preceded the decline of the area, residents perceived it as a threat and there was considerable potential for conflict. On the other hand, where, as in Moss Side, the decline in status of the area preceded the arrival of the immigrants, the level of conflict was much less, and there was potential for a shared perception of the problems of the area. This was manifested in Moss Side by the existence of a number of protest movements of multi-racial composition against the city council over shared housing interests. The second feature Ward identified was the economic base of the cities in which the immigrants arrived. In this context he stresses the importance of the particular reasons for the influx of immigrants. Coloured immigrants came to Britain to meet shortages of labour in sections of the labour market which had become unattractive as white workers moved to more attractive and better paid jobs. The demand for such workers existed in many parts of Britain, both growing and declining. Ward argues that the arrival of immigrants will have a different impact in cities with a growing manufacturing base, such as Birmingham was in the 1960s, with a high level of in-migration of white workers, and consequently considerable pressure on the housing market; second, in a declining area; and third, in metropolitan areas where growth in the tertiary sector was replacing declining traditional industries, of which Manchester was a case. He argues that in the last type of area there would be considerable economic opportunities for immigrants, and less pressure on the housing market from white immigrants.

Can patterns explain patterns?

The very different experiences of immigrants in different cities shows that on their own particular patterns in space can show nothing about the life chances of individuals living in particular areas. Do we have to conclude from the fact that case studies in different areas produce different results that all cities are different, and that it is therefore impossible to make useful general statements about the process and structures of urban life?

We saw at the beginning of this chapter that attempts were made to explain what went on in cities in terms of areas with specific functions and ecological processes which assigned different people to these areas. This approach has been rightly criticised for claiming to provide a universal explanation applying to all cities. At the most basic level, we would expect different processes to operate in cities in societies with different economic systems. For example, we would expect urban life to be very different in East and West Berlin, even though they are in some sense part of the same city. In all cities the detail is important. The distinctions in terms of function say nothing about what sort of people fulfil these functions. It will make a difference if segregation is between black and white people or between Catholic and Protestant, or if no ethnic division exists. It will make a considerable difference if the city is growing, with many immigrants, or is stagnating, with people tending to leave. This point leads on to a more serious criticism of the ecological approach: that it seeks to find explanations internal to the city, when the city is in fact being subjected to outside processes. An analogy for the ecologists' emphasis on the interconnection of different elements in the urban system is life in a pond. The analogy shows the dangers of the approach, since many had the false idea that the competition between organisms in the pond created the climate, rather than the other way round.

The change in the title of this book since the first edition twelve years ago reflects a major shift in the focus of urban sociology from the study of patterns of urban life, which were seen as operating autonomously within the city, to a study of wider social processes and structures whose impact is seen in the city. These same twelve years have seen a shift in Britain from economic growth to economic decline. In this climate of decline, it is manifest that what goes on in the city is determined by outside processes. Nevertheless, it is still worth studying the city, since it is an important index of the effect of wider social and economic processes. To return to the pond analogy, there is a case for looking at the pond as a way of detecting secular changes in the climate. If the water level gradually declines from year to year, or certain species disappear through winter cold, or the greater concentration of nutrients in the summer, longer-term climatic oscillations may be perceived.

A few of the wider processes to which we are referring may be mentioned. They will be developed and added to in subsequent chapters. Decisions which government makes on the level of public spending and the appropriate balance between public and private investment have crucial effects on the housing and services people can obtain and also the jobs that are available. Trends in the world market will affect the profitability of the main industries of a city, and hence the chances of expansion or contraction of employment. Government planning and taxation policies may at one time favour industrial investment, and at another property speculation, with important implications for employment and the physical form of the city. Shifts in the price and supply of world energy resources will determine transport costs and hence the pattern of development of a city. These processes and others are of far greater significance in determining local geographical patterns than forces which are endogenous to the area.

It is important to understand the operation of these common processes affecting all cities, but it is equally important to recognise that they do not have common results in all cities. The impact of economic change is not uniform in space or across social groups. In a period of decline, there are still some groups and some areas which are benefiting; in a period of growth there are still some groups and some areas which are losing. Even among those who are losing, it makes a difference whether you are employed in an area where there are opportunities to supplement income through informal work or in places where there are none. The urban needs to be seen as a set of possibilities which are structured. What you can do in a city is set within constraints imposed by outside processes, but these constraints are different in different cities. Each locality is a mosaic of opportunities and constraints resulting from the varying responses to external forces.

4

THE HOUSING MARKET

Introduction

Evidently one of the most important aspects of people's everyday lives is their housing. Housing performs a number of different functions; it provides shelter, safety and privacy; it is used as a commodity to realise income and wealth through the system of private property ownership; and it may represent a symbol of social status. Moreover, a house has a specific physical location and this will determine the other urban facilities, such as schools and jobs, to which the resident has access. Housing, therefore, is not just a physical element in the built environment, but can also be conceptualised as a social resource which involves complex social relationships. It is with these social relations that we are primarily concerned.

People attempt to meet their housing needs within given social structures – the opportunities and the constraints on access to housing. This approach highlights the segregation of the housing market between tenure groups – between those who buy their houses and those who rent them. It also shows that once people are in different housing tenure groups, they are likely to experience differences in housing standards, in more general life-chances and in political interests. However, before looking at tenure in more detail we will consider the physical housing stock, since the nature of the housing physically available is the first constraint on what housing people can get.

The housing stock

Because housing is relatively expensive to produce, and lasts for a long time, the housing market is always made up of an inherited stock of dwellings with physical characteristics which cannot be rapidly changed. There are variations in types of dwellings, age, space and facilities, both within and between tenures, and the housing stock will vary considerably between different areas.

In absolute terms, the number of dwellings (i.e. houses, flats, bedsits, etc.) has risen from about 16.5 million in 1960 to 19.5 million in 1971 and 21.1 million in 1978. This increase in the number of dwellings is the net result of gains from new buildings and conversions, and losses after demolition through slum clearance.

In simple numerical terms, the housing stock had moved from a situation of deficit in 1961 to one of surplus by 1971, and there are now more dwellings than households. This global surplus, however, is misleading, because much of the stock is inadequate and old, and because it is not the quantity of housing available which is problematic, but its quality, distribution and availability in appropriate forms, in specific locations for particular needs. Vacant buildings, lack of amenities, overcrowding and sharing all pose difficulties which are ignored by a narrow concentration on numbers alone. Moreover, probably the most important changes have been in the numbers of dwellings in different tenures, because this affects the structure of the housing market as a whole. In 1971 owner-occupied dwellings made up 50 percent of the housing market; 31 percent were rented from local authorities and new towns, dwellings rented from private landlords made up 14 percent, and the remaining 5 percent were other tenures, such as dwellings tied to a job. Since then, owner-occupation has expanded rapidly and local authority renting has increased more slowly, while private renting and other tenures have steadily diminished. We shall examine these trends in more detail later, but we must now look at the indicators of the standard or quality of our housing.

Regional variations

Housing problems take on a different form in different areas. For example, in older urban areas and inner cities the main difficulty may be the physical deterioration of the housing stock through obsolescence, whereas in other areas it is the limited supply of accommodation which causes public concern. The processes of industrialisation, urbanisation and uneven regional development outlined in Chapters 1 and 2 alert us to the historical and geographic dimensions of housing problems. Indeed, we argue that simply by living in one part of the country rather than another, people encounter different housing opportunities and experiences. Thus there is no simple sense in which we can speak of a unified national housing market.

A comparison of the tenure breakdown between regions reveals noticeable differences. Thus, in 1971, the proportion of the regional housing stock owner-occupied varied from 58 percent in the South-West, to 42 percent in the Northern region, and 30 percent in Scotland. Conversely, housing rented from local authorities varied from 24 percent in the South-West, to 38 percent in the North, and 52 percent in Scotland. Private rented accommodation shows less regional variation, but there are still important differences. The outcome of these regional patterns in tenure is that the structure of local housing markets, and thus the degree of choice or constraint on access, is far from uniform. In other words, the interrelationship between where you live and the structure of housing opportunities is crucial.

There is considerable variation in the standards and condition of housing, and a substantial minority of dwellings are unsatisfactory, either because they lack basic amenities, such as a fixed bath or inside WC, or because they are structurally unsound. There has been a steady decline in the number of unsatisfactory dwellings. It is estimated that the number of dwellings classified as unfit or lacking basic amenities fell from 4.7 million in 1961 to 1.9 million in 1971. Similarly, the number of *households* lacking exclusive use of an inside WC fell from 2.3 million in 1971 to 1.2 million in 1977. Nevertheless, there is evidence that in spite of improvements, there are still sections of the population living in inadequate housing, and that they are unevenly distributed between tenure groups and between areas. Thus, the 1.7 million dwellings classified as 'physically unsatisfactory' in 1976 were disproportionately concentrated in the privately rented sector, so that while 5.7 percent of owner-occupied and 6.3 percent of local authority dwellings were defined as unsatisfactory, 29.6

percent of other tenures (mostly private rented) were so described. Within a seemingly small or residual proportion of inadequate housing, it is striking that the private rented sector still contains the worst accommodation.

Turning to regional and local variations, the spatial concentration of very poor housing is obvious in certain districts, especially older inner city areas. For example, in 1971 in Tyneside, about 12 percent of households did not have a fixed bath and 17 percent lacked an inside toilet. In Merseyside, the proportions were 11 percent and 16 percent respectively, compared to a national average of 8 percent and 11 percent. Even within tenure groups there are regional variations in the possession of basic amenities like an inside toilet, hot water supply and fixed bath. Thus, for example, amongst owner-occupiers there were 9 percent in East Anglia, 7 percent in West Yorkshire and 3 percent in Greater London who lacked a fixed bath in 1971. The proportions of households lacking facilities are much higher among private renters, but again 41 percent of households renting unfurnished private accommodation in Tyneside were without a fixed bath, 35 percent in West Yorkshire and 27 percent in Greater London. Generally, local authority housing does not vary so dramatically between regions.

The significance of tenure

Tenure is probably the single most important variable in any analysis of the housing market and, as we have already seen, it differentiates both types of housing and types of household. The term tenure is quasi-legal and refers to the status of a householder *vis-à-vis* his housing and, specifically, his legal rights regarding ownership and/or the conditions and obligations of residence. Sociologically, tenure is important because it expresses the structural differentiation of social groups in the housing market and is determined by social, economic and political relations, as we shall see when we discuss 'housing class'. Tenure affects the right to buy or sell the property and to modify the structure; it affects legal rights over payment of rent or other charges, and dispossession, eviction and compensation.

Major changes in the pattern of housing tenure have occurred in the last twenty years, but these form part of longer historic trends. At the beginning of the First World War only a small fraction of the population was in owner-occupation and the huge majority rented privately. By the 1940s about one-third of the population was in owner-occupation, a small minority were council tenants, and the remainder private tenants. After the last war the trend for increased owner-occupation and local authority renting accelerated, and the private rented sector progressively declined. These developments are, of course, inter-connected and the explanation of these changes is complex.

The growth of owner-occupation has been encouraged by general economic growth and the increased desire and ability of people to purchase their own homes. Governments of both parties have supported this trend, and the expansion of the building societies and taxation advantages assisted the funding of house buying. On the other hand, local authority housing has been expanded in an attempt to meet the needs of groups unable to afford to buy houses, and/or who live in unsatisfactory accommodation or slum clearance areas. Council housing has received central government subsidies, but has been subject to changing political priorities at national and local levels. The private rented sector has been affected by several factors and its decline is due to a combination of legislation about security for tenants and rent controls, the prospect of better forms of investment elsewhere for landlords, the effects of urban renewal and changing preferences with greater demand for owner-occupation or council housing. Many privately rented houses have thus been 'converted' by selling into owner-occupation or have been demolished in slum clearance.

Tenure categories are sometimes referred to as 'sub-markets' or sectors of the total housing market, and this reflects the different procedures for allocation and access within each tenure. The examination of these different sub-markets is a major step in the task of analysing the links between housing and the social structure generally, and social class in particular. These class differences remain fundamentally linked to the work that people do and the inequalities of this relationship are relatively unchanging. We will begin by showing the marked differences in social class composition of different tenure groups, and will then look

TABLE 4.1 *Tenure by socio-economic group, 1975*

	Owner Occupied (%)	Renting from local authority (%)
Professionals, employers and managers	80	8
Intermediate non-manual employees	58.5	22
Skilled manual workers	49	36
Semi-skilled workers	35	45
Unskilled workers	20	59

Source: *Housing Policy – Technical Volume*, Department of the Environment, HMSO 1977, p. 83

in more detail at the processes in each tenure which lead to this outcome.

There is a considerable theoretical debate about the concept of social class, but if we use the conventional definitions of socio-economic group based on occupation, a clear picture does emerge. Table 4.1 shows the percentage of each socio-economic group in owner-occupation and renting from local authorities. There is a clear relationship, therefore, between social class (or socio-economic group) and tenure: owner-occupation is the dominant tenure among the middle class, and council renting the major tenure for working class households.

Over the last twenty years, as the private rented sector has diminished, there has been a corresponding increase in the proportion of both non-manual and manual workers in owner-occupation, as well as a parallel rise in the proportion of manual workers in local authority accommodation. There appears to have been some 'convergence' between the intermediate non-manual employees and skilled manual workers in their housing situation. Nevertheless, despite this overlap, there is still a disparity at the extremes of the social class hierarchy. We can conclude that the degree of social class polarisation in housing tenure has been modified, but it remains significant and substantial. Incomes are, of course, directly related to social class through occupational earnings and the range of incomes within tenures is a further indication of the links between tenure and social class, but it is also significant in its own right. The data used here refer only to heads of households working or seeking

TABLE 4.2 Tenure by income of head of household, Great Britain, 1978

| Head of household's annual income | Owner occupiers | | Tenants | | | Sample |
	Outright owners	Mortgagors	Local authority	Unfurnished private	Furnished private	(Nos.)
Up to £2,000	17	8	49	19	7	467
£2,000 but under £3,000	14	21	46	15	4	1,085
£3,000 but under £4,000	13	37	38	10	2	1,767
£4,000 but under £5,000	11	52	28	8	2	1,376
£5,000 and over	15	66	12	6	1	1,489

Source: *Social Trends*, **10** (1980) p. 199

work in formal paid employment. In Table 4.2 we can see a more or less regular rank-order, with the highest income earners in owner-occupation, followed by intermediate earners in local authority housing, and then lower income groups over-represented in unfurnished private tenancies.

Generally, high income correlates with owner-occupation and low incomes are common among council tenants. But there is a considerable number of outright owners on low incomes and these are usually elderly households, or owners who have bought very poor quality, cheap housing in older urban areas. There are also some local authority households with relatively large incomes, particularly since these households are more likely to contain more than one earner. Nevertheless, the local authority sector also contains a large and growing proportion of poor people, and an increasing proportion (57 per cent) of all households receiving Supplementary Benefit.

Reviewing these variations in income by tenure, we can see that house buyers are considerably better off than other housing consumers. Moreover, the effect of recent trends has been to steadily increase the segregation of households by income between the two major sectors. Nevertheless, the largest proportion of skilled manual workers is now in owner-occupation, so the issue of mobility through the housing market and access to different tenures requires further investigation. We need to know how people enter and leave different housing situations and which factors influence the accessibility of different tenures, in order to understand the dynamics of housing. For these reasons we now turn to an analysis of the processes of access and allocation in the housing market.

Access to housing: constraints and opportunities

In the private sector of the housing market housing is essentially a commodity. This means that land owners, property developers, builders, surveyors, architects, estate agents, solicitors and (in a special sense) building societies are all engaged in the business of producing and distributing a scarce resource for profit. Landlords, house-buyers and sellers 'use' their accommodation, but are also caught up in the financial network of the market when they purchase and subsequently realise the capital value of their asset. In the public sector housing is in principle produced and allocated on the basis of 'social need', rather than ability to pay the price. However, the provision of council housing entails the purchase of land, construction and administration costs, and finance has to be obtained from state and private sources.

Thus, financial considerations are very important in the public and private sectors, and a major determinant of access to housing. However, in both sectors there are also social processes which determine access. In both private and public sectors institutions ration and allocate housing and their operations have an important influence. They complicate the link between social class and tenure, since the formal and informal rules used mean that factors such as race, gender and family composition also determine housing position. We will now examine the financial context and the means of access for each tenure category.

The private rented sector

The private rented sector can be regarded as a sub-market in which landlords lease or rent accommodation to tenants for payment, with the aim of securing an economic return on their investment. Private renting is an investment which may or may not secure an economic return. For many years, however, there has been state regulation of this sector to control the level of rents charged and to give certain categories of tenant legal rights of occupancy or security of tenure. As a group, landlords are not eligible for tax relief for interest payments on mortgages and must pay tax on income received from rents. These factors, together with the cost of property repair and maintenance and the availability of other more profitable sources for investment, have contributed to the decrease in private lettings. Moreover, the financial pressures on landlords mean that they have little incentive to invest in maintenance and improvement, as a result of which the worst housing conditions tend to be found in this sector.

At the same time as these legal regulations have reduced the supply of housing in this sector, the demand has not declined to anything like the same extent. This results from the fact that it caters largely for groups who are unable to enter other tenures, either through low income or failure to meet local authority eligibility criteria, and hence is subject to intense competition between consumers. In a situation of high demand, tenants' ability to pay remains the overriding determinant of access to rented accommodation and the conditions and facilities that it contains.

However, there are factors other than the ability to pay which constrain access. Landlords themselves or their agents control entry to their property and may decide upon their own rules for access and eligibility, which may involve evaluations of social status as well as income. Informal selection and exclusion practices may result in effective discrimination against certain social groups; for example, ethnic minorities. This is doubly significant because private renting is often the *only* form of housing available to certain people, since they are unable to buy and/or are ineligible for council housing. Although there are different submarkets within the private rented sector catering for different demands (for example, some people prefer to rent privately because of job mobility), exclusion from other tenures and restrictions on access within the sector impose *constraints* on private tenants.

Public sector housing

Inability to pay is very rarely a constraint on access to local authority housing, but financial considerations do still impinge, since they determine the supply of housing. In addition, the operation of bureaucratic methods of allocating local authority housing has important effects on this sub-market. Historically, some housing has been provided by public authorities for special categories of people since the end of the nineteenth century. Originally, state intervention in housing was concerned with fears about public health (due to the insanitary conditions and overcrowding) and the need to provide accommodation for the industrial working class. Legislation subsequently imposed the duty on councils to provide housing for people made homeless by slum clearance and those living in overcrowded and insanitary conditions. Even now, however, statutory requirements are imprecise, since local authorities are merely obliged to *consider* the housing needs of their district and there is no compulsion to provide a specific amount of housing.

Nevertheless, central government has sought to encourage local councils to build housing and has devised a complex loan subsidy system to finance the construction of local authority dwellings. Money from central government, from loans borrowed on the financial market, and from tenants' rents and other rates revenue is used by councils to buy and service land and to pay for construction, maintenance and administrative costs. It is not surprising to learn that rent charges, interest payments on loans and the levels of subsidy are all matters of political dispute within and between central and local government. Thus, the rate of council house building is directly affected by national policies on public expenditure as well as local political attitudes.

Conflicts between political parties extend beyond the amount of exchequer subsidy to include in council housing rents. Generally, council tenants pay rents which are lower than would apply in the 'open market' and less than the real cost of their home. Authorities 'pool' the rents for their whole stock, so that the individual dwelling rents do not have to reflect the 'historic' cost of that dwelling, which would otherwise vary with age. Rates and subsidies are used to balance the difference between actual costs and rental income, but different authorities adopt different policies with the consequence that there is wide variation in rents between councils.

Local authority housing allocation. Entry to council housing is influenced by a complex set of factors. In principle, tenancies are allocated 'bureaucratically'; that is, on the basis of priority needs determined by a 'points' scheme. Applicants on a waiting list receive points according to their personal and family socio-economic circumstances, current housing situation and sometimes official (but informal) evaluations of their merit or desert. Household size, age of the applicant, current health and housing conditions may all be included in a council's calculation of housing need. Other primary criteria include residence requirements or employment in the local authority area (often for a fixed period), income and present housing tenure. However, meeting these criteria does not guarantee access to council housing: they are preliminary rules to determine *eligibility* for consideration as potential tenants.

Local authorities have considerable discretion in deciding

what their housing priorities are, and in administering their allocation procedures. There is wide variation in eligibility criteria and in the rules for allocating specific tenancies to applicants, for exchanges or for transfers. Access to council tenancies is not therefore simply a matter of fulfilling technical or bureaucratic regulations, but entails social encounters where implicit criteria of evaluation may be used by officials to determine the 'suitability' of a tenant.

Placement within the council stock is further affected by informal selection processes when 'good' tenants are rewarded with desirable properties in popular estates, whereas 'problem families' may be penalised through allocation of a hard-to-let flat on an unpopular estate. Thus, in the determination of housing needs in the local authority sector there is a social process of categorisation, labelling and management underlying the formal procedures and objective indices. Some households may fit the prevailing criteria for access, and others may not: in both cases, their housing opportunities are directly affected in invidious ways. Thus, access to local authority housing is determined by both financial and bureaucratic considerations. The ability to get a house will depend on the total supply, which may vary over time, with central government policy, and between authorities. It will also depend on meeting the criteria for allocation which tend to select some groups and exclude others.

Owner-occupation

Owning your own home usually involves the purchase of the building and the land on which it stands. Most housing is extremely expensive as a commodity in relation to normal earnings, and so it is rare for someone to be able to afford to buy his home outright (unless he is wealthy or the house is very cheap). The majority of house-buyers must purchase through a long-term loan or mortgage, but they are usually aware that this is a worthwhile investment. Indeed, housing is generally regarded as a good investment because inflation ensures that the real cost of a mortgage debt declines while the value of the asset increases. In addition, house-buyers receive tax relief for interest charges on their mortgage.

Eventually, therefore, owners of houses can accrue wealth

through capital gains on the sale of their property. Even though buying another house may entail paying a higher price, the increase in market value of the original house usually provides a 'profit' for reinvestment. Consequently, owner-occupation is an important source of wealth during people's life-times and, of course, such property wealth can be transmitted through inheritance. According to the recent Royal Commission on wealth, home ownership actually comprises a major element in the overall distribution of personal wealth: in 1960, houses owned by people accounted for 19 percent of total personal wealth, but this had increased to 37 percent in 1976.

The building societies. Raising the finance to cover the purchase price is probably the first major difficulty confronting prospective house-buyers. Credit is available from a variety of sources: apart from family, friends and other private sources, the bulk of mortgages is provided by local authorities, insurance companies, banks and, above all, building societies. Britain is distinctive in having not only such a large proportion of owner-occupiers, but also in having the majority of house-buying finance provided by one major institution – the building societies. They have directly encouraged the rapid expansion of owner-occupation.

The dominance of building societies is shown in recent data for the UK: in 1978, 91 percent of all mortgages were advanced by building societies, 6 percent by local authorities and 3 percent by insurance companies. The tendency has been for building societies to increase their role as principal financiers of house purchase at the expense of other agencies, and they control a vast and growing proportion of finance for house purchase.

The dominance of the building societies is significant because they control entry into the housing market through their rules about mortgage allocation. Raising a mortgage essentially depends on two things – the 'quality' of the applicant and the 'quality' of the property, because there is a risk attached to both in the eyes of the lender. Both aspects thus affect access to owner-occupation.

Applications for building society mortgages are generally dealt with at local branch offices: decisions are authorised by branch managers, but funds are allocated nationally or regionally within the society, with certain categories of applicant receiving priority. Applicants basically have to satisfy income and occupational requirements related to the risk of defaulting on mortgage repayments. Thus, an income quotient is used to fix the amount of loan and incomes must be sufficient to support repayments and be perceived to be stable and secure. Clearly, social class and status considerations enter into these assessments, and certain groups (for example, less skilled manual workers and all women workers) may find themselves at a disadvantage, if not effectively excluded from the outset.

The property itself is also relevant since it is the security for the loan. Building societies fix the amount of mortgage not only on the basis of applicant's income, but also in relation to the type, age, condition and location of the house and may offer a loan up to a given percentage of *their* valuation (not necessarily the purchase price), for a named period and with conditions (e.g. repairs) imposed. Any shortfall between the mortgage and purchase price has to be made up from the purchaser's savings, and often building societies insist on a minimum savings deposit and/or require that borrowers should invest with the society prior to their mortgage application.

Another important effect of building societies' operations is relevant to our discussion of access, and that is their impact on the *types* of property considered for lending. On the whole, building societies have been reluctant to lend on older terraced or unmodernised property, favouring instead modern medium-priced houses. The consequences are that people wanting mortgages on cheaper, older houses (almost certainly low income groups) find it difficult to obtain building society funds, and are forced to turn to other financial sources, including fringe banks (this applies to ethnic minority groups especially). In addition to this, whole tracts of inner urban areas become effectively deprived of investment, which contributes to the deterioration of the housing stock.

Thus, access in owner-occupation is mediated by various institutions, and allocation is at the discretion of certain private sector 'gatekeepers' or 'urban managers'. The effect of their practices is to favour some social groups (conventional families with high income earners in stable jobs) as well as certain forms of housing (semi-detached suburban or new houses). The housing market is made up of elaborate constraints which limit, exclude and discriminate, and house-buyers (like all other housing consumers) have to negotiate their way through these constraints. However, despite these barriers, owner-occupation has become the major tenure: access to it confers economic, legal and symbolic benefits which are not available in other tenures.

Housing classes

We have seen in previous sections the ways in which housing is differentiated physically, and we have shown major social and economic differences between people in different tenures. The housing market is clearly associated with inequalities of access, condition and opportunity between social groups, and we must consider the implications of these inequalities. What we wish to stress is that people have varying abilities to determine their own housing 'careers', and that the factors which define 'routes' through the housing market are not solely economic. Thus, the structure of opportunities available in housing is a product of both market and bureaucratic processes operating within a social and spatial system.

This kind of approach has developed out of discussions of the concept of 'housing class' and it has given rise to much theoretical and empirical argument. The idea of housing classes was first developed by the sociologists John Rex and Robert Moore (1967) in their study of race relations and housing in an inner area of Birmingham. They observed that housing was a scarce resource in the inner city and that competition in the market for access to domestic property was modified by the presence of the public sector. A link with the Weberian theory of stratification was made because Weber had argued that ownership of domestic property was just as significant as ownership of industrial capital in class formation. Rex and Moore indeed suggested that there was a class struggle over the use of housing and that this was the central process of the city as a social unit. They argued that individuals in the same position in the job market may still have differential degrees of access to housing depending on such factors as their length of residence, colour of skin pigmentation, access to capital, number of dependants, and so on. The following are the housing classes distinguished by Rex and Moore:

1 the outright owners of large houses in desirable areas;
2 mortgage payers who 'own' whole houses in desirable areas;
3 council tenants in council-built houses;
4 council tenants in slum houses awaiting demolition;
5 tenants of a whole house owned by a private landlord;
6 owners of houses bought with short-term loans who are compelled to let rooms in order to meet their repayment obligations;
7 tenants of rooms in a lodging house.

These housing classes are arranged in a hierarchy of prestige or status and will follow a definite territorial distribution in the city, dependent on the age and size of the buildings. They also argue that membership of a housing class had significant effects on life-chances, interests and life-style. The crucial point in Rex and Moore's analysis is that, although the labour market largely determines individuals' positions and power in the housing market, other factors make it possible for a person to occupy *different* class positions in relation to his job and housing.

Among the most important criticisms of the housing class model is Haddon's objection that current position in the housing market is the *outcome* of market or class inequality rather than its cause (Haddon 1970). The issue highlighted here is that people actually living in one tenure do not have equal chances of moving to other tenures: some may be in a better or worse position and thus have different potentials for improving their housing position. Again, the importance of access emerges, and a stress on the route, method or means by which people enter or leave a housing tenure.

Pahl had pointed out that the possession of capital was probably the most important variable determining access (Pahl 1975, p. 245). However, this does not deal with the fact that within the group who are forced to rent because they lack capital there are other important social differences and constraints; for example, their failure to meet council housing eligibility requirements. Thus Lambert, Paris and Blackaby (1978, pp. 6–8) have argued that Pahl's account neglects the special conditions affecting access to local authority housing; and Rex and Tomlinson

(1979, pp. 128–29) have also emphasised that different kinds of renting reflect an unequal distribution of power in the housing market. We acknowledge this important qualification and agree that in both the public *and* private sectors it is the *means of access* and/or the rules of eligibility which produce structural divisions between housing consumers, whether or not we wish to designate such groups as distinctive housing classes.

Nevertheless, Saunders (1979, Ch. 2) maintains that it *is* possible to use a Weberian approach to housing to identify housing classes. He argues that class position in relation to domestic property is critically affected by the basic division between owners and non-owners. The possibility of deriving a return from the sale of housing gives owners a unique advantage over other tenure groups: owners have the right and capacity to use their property to realise wealth, whereas other groups cannot. For Saunders, if a housing situation entails the potential to generate income through disposal of property in a market, then (following Weber) it must be regarded as the basis for class formation.

In his analysis of owner-occupation, Saunders makes three points. Firstly, because house price inflation has increased at a faster rate than general inflation, the costs of house purchase have increased, so benefiting existing owners, who possess an appreciating asset. Secondly, people with mortgages generally have cheap credit in the long-term since they borrow money at relatively low interest levels. Thirdly, people with mortgages benefit through tax relief on interest charges, so they receive an indirect subsidy from the state.

It is these aspects of home owning which enable owners to accumulate wealth, albeit through a kind of 'involuntary saving', and thus owner-occupation represents a form of investment unavailable to other housing consumers. Therefore, as Pahl (1975, p. 291) has remarked elsewhere, owner-occupier families 'may gain more from the housing market in a few years than would be possible in savings from a lifetime of earnings'.

The implication of this is that there is an *objective* conflict of interests between owner-occupiers and renters because of their fundamentally different housing class positions. However, Dunleavy has argued that *politically* the division of interests is not between home-owners and all renters or non-owners, but between home-owners and council tenants, and he shows that housing tenure has a significant effect on party allegiances independent of social class. Dunleavy (1979) traces this cleavage to state subsidies to each sector (tax relief on mortgages and local authority housing expenditure) and disputes about equity in the distribution of these subsidies. Housing policy is currently the subject of intense party political debate, and government decisions about subsidies to the two sectors can make a considerable difference to people's incomes and life-chances.

Whatever the exact boundaries of cleavage between housing consumers, conflict over housing is obviously important in the social structure and in the everyday experience of individuals and families. For this reason, Rex and Tomlinson (1979, Ch. 5) have re-emphasised the value of the concept of housing class. Although they acknowledge that conflicts over housing are one of a number of *interrelated* forms of social class conflict, they maintain that, empirically, wherever there is a housing stock of varying desirability and whenever there are different social groups with unequal access to that housing, housing classes can be identified.

Conclusion

Evidently, access to housing is unequal and the structure of housing opportunities encountered by some groups is inferior to that enjoyed by others. Inequality in the housing market, however, is not simply the result of the uneven distribution of income, capital or credit-worthiness, because other social factors determine eligibility for public and private sector tenancies. Some people successfully negotiate the rules, procedures and gatekeepers and are able to raise credit or buy or rent accommodation which they prefer. Others are unable to purchase (and are unlikely to in the future), but satisfy entrance criteria for local authority tenancies which they may or may not desire. Yet other groups are excluded from these tenures and are forced to rent inferior housing while still finding it difficult to gain access to other tenures. Thus, within a housing position the chances of *exit* are also unequal: the options and avenues open to owner-occupiers, for example, are certainly superior to those of the council tenant.

The emphasis of this chapter has been on local agencies such as councils and building societies, but we must not forget that too close a focus on the rules of the game may lead us to neglect the question of why the game is being played at all. More precisely, it may lead us to neglect the fact that capitalist relations underlie the behaviour of all the institutions with which we have been concerned. The largest part of the housing market is in a form which stresses the accumulation of private property and only a residual part purports to be based on social need. Even in this sector provision depends on economic decisions outside the control of those providing the housing; for example, the terms on which councils can raise capital. Thus we can see a direct link between housing and the major institutional framework of the economy.

Earlier sections of this chapter described the pattern of changes in our housing stock and showed the increasing dominance of owner-occupation, the minority role of public sector housing and the residual nature of private renting. We noted that there are marked differences in physical conditions, facilities and the extent of overcrowding between tenures. The two major tenures were shown to be socially polarised between working and middle class groups, and financial and other accessibility criteria were found to be related to this pattern. Finally, we considered the usefulness of the concept of 'housing class' and concluded that it does direct our attention to categories of people whose housing opportunities cannot be directly inferred from their position in the job market alone. We now turn to the wider relevance of labour markets for our understanding of urban life.

5

THE LOCAL LABOUR MARKET

Unless one has inherited wealth, one has to earn money by getting a job. In contemporary industrial society, most people offer their labour or skill in return for a wage or salary. This is all very obvious, but how is the match between the wage and the labour to be fixed? According to neo-classical economic theory, there is a labour market containing freely competing individuals with complete information about opportunities and in which there are no obstacles to the adjustment of supply and demand through the price mechanisms. However, this model of the labour market does not bear any resemblance to reality. There are major constraints and limits on access to jobs.

In this chapter we emphasise that labour markets are generally limited in space. Some labour markets, to be sure, operate on a world scale and atomic physicists, for example, might move between Harwell and California more easily than the school caretaker could move thirty miles away. But it would be wrong to see labour markets decreasing in scale as skill is reduced. In many industrial societies over the past thirty years it has been the *least* skilled workers who have come from long distances – from Turkey to Germany, from the West Indies to Britain, or from Algeria to France. However, most people expect to find work within an easy journey from home. This poses serious constraints on opportunities and this will be the main focus of this chapter, because position in the labour market is a fundamental determinant of life-chances.

Job opportunities in local labour markets vary substantially across the country, depending on the location of different industries. Thus people's income and life choices are crucially influenced by where they live. Moreover, the opportunities in local labour markets are continually changing with the rise and fall of different industries. The central problem is that new industry does not replace the older declining industry in the same location. New high technology industries do not start up in the mill towns of Lancashire, which were prosperous a century ago but have declined with the textile industry, nor even in the West Midlands where the car industry has grown over the last fifty years but is now in decline. Instead, they start in prosperous areas such as the Upper Thames valley. These processes of change in local labour markets will be caused by factors which are completely outside local control, such as changing patterns of investment by large companies and changes in world trade.

However, this spatial differentiation is only one of the ways in which labour markets are limited. There are other differentiating dimensions which are equally important. Some writers have identified what is labelled as a 'dual labour market'. The primary labour market contains jobs which are relatively secure, highly skilled and well paid. Workers have access to promotion ladders and tend to be well protected by trade unions and professional associations. By contrast, in the secondary labour market turnover is high, wages are relatively low, fewer skills are demanded, prospects of promotion are negligible, and trade unions are weak or non-existent. The secondary labour market contains a high proportion of women workers, ethnic minorities and the young.

A German sociologist, Reinhard Kreckel, has identified an even more detailed segmentation of the labour market depending on the market situations of groups of workers. This distinguishes between workers with general skills, and those with skills which are specific to an individual company who have few chances of mobility, between workers whose skills are in demand because of technological change, and those whose skills are undermined by this change, and between groups who can effectively limit the supply of workers with their skills and those who cannot exercise this strategy of 'social closure'. These forms of differentiation of the labour market in space and by skill level lead to a form of structured *social* inequality in space.

The spatial distribution of employment

The spatial inequalities between labour markets can most easily be seen from the variation in the level of unemployment. Even in 1968, when the UK average unemployment rate was 2.5 percent, the rates in the different regions varied between 1.6 percent in the South-East and 4.6 percent in the North. The substantial rise in national unemployment rates in the early 1980s has led to even more marked regional variations. Thus, in May 1981, when the unemployment rate for the whole UK was 10.6 percent, the rate in the North was 14.1 percent, that in Wales was 13.7 percent, in Scotland 12.7 percent and in Northern Ireland 17.6 percent. Within regions there are areas with even higher levels of unemployment. Most seriously affected are the inner areas of large cities. For example, in 1981 the unemployment rate in Liverpool was 16.7 percent. Even within prosperous regions, there can be pockets of high unemployment. Thus, the Isle of Sheppey in the South-East had an unemployment rate of 18 percent in 1981. Within areas of high unemployment some social groups, such as ethnic minorities and the young, are particularly badly affected.

These spatial inequalities have persisted over very long periods, and the regions noted above have had relatively high unemployment rates since the 1920s. The peripheral regions have shown slower growth of total employment, lower incomes, higher unemployment and more net outmigration of populations than the economically prosperous or buoyant regions. Thus, the chances of getting a job vary between regions and areas. The inequalities reflect the historical pattern of uneven regional economic development and changing rates of economic expansion.

However, some writers claim that the current unemployment problem is not adequately defined in territorial terms. Despite the gaps between the South-East and the rest of the country, the vast disparities of the 1930s are not now apparent. At least one economist has recently argued that today a person's prospects in the labour market depend as much on his occupation and age as on the area where he lives. Now the major issue is the growth of long-term unemployment among *manual* workers: differences between social classes are becoming as important as differences between places in determining employment opportunities.

We have seen that problems which are experienced locally do not have local solutions, but government has persisted in maintaining that measures offering local inducement to industry in areas of high unemployment will serve to regenerate their local economies. Government regional policy since the 1930s has offered a variety of such inducements, such as the construction of factories, subsidies for employment and tax relief in investment. It has also attempted to regulate industrial growth in the prosperous regions.

There has been considerable dispute about the effectiveness of these measures. Some economists argue that they have been effective in creating jobs, but the fact remains that large interregional inequalities have persisted for decades despite government policies.

Some writers deny that regional policy even had as its main aim the creation of employment in the regions. Thus Pickvance (1981) has argued that regional policy has been a means of providing state support to subsidise industrial capital in a period of falling profits. He claims that reducing unemployment was at best a secondary policy goal – the primary concern being the provision of incentives and benefits to modern capital-intensive firms.

Population migration

Governments have also suggested, in addition to regional policy, that workers should move to other labour markets in order to maximise their social and economic opportunities. In spite of the obvious benefits of moving workers to where there are jobs available, there are some negative effects of migration. Obviously, mobile young skilled workers leaving an already declining area may hasten the deterioration of the economic base there and increase the ratio of the dependent population. However, immigrants in areas of economic growth may generate some local economic multiplier effects in the labour market, but they may also cause further pressure on the housing market and put greater demands on public infrastructure and services.

It would seem that the amount of migration which has actually taken place has been rather lower than might have been antici- pated. In the last thirty years there has been a considerable volume of migration, but only a minority of movements relate to people changing their jobs. Most movements are over a short distance and take place because people want to change their housing, rather than their jobs. The long distance moves have led to some gain in population in the South and Midlands at the expense of the North and other industrial areas; and smaller towns, particularly new towns with newer high technology in- dustries, have grown at the expense of the conurbations.

However, there still remain areas where labour is in demand along with areas of high unemployment, so we have to look for reasons why people do not or cannot move. There are strong pressures on people against moving for job reasons which we may divide into two related sets of *constraints on migration*. First, movement, particularly over the distances generally necessary to change jobs, involves social upheaval and disruption of kinship and friendship networks. There is often a general reluctance to leave the home area for a strange environment. Although this ap- plies to all social groups, there are social class differences in the propensity to move. Age and stage of the life-cycle obviously affect the decision to move too.

Second, there is a range of constraints related to the housing market. Owner-occupiers may face difficulties in buying or sell- ing a house. The financial costs of moving, such as removal ex- penses and legal fees, may be considerable. There are also sub- stantial variations in house prices across the country; for exam- ple, in early 1981 average prices varied between £18,068 in the Northern region and £29,631 in the South-East. These differ- ences occur across all house types. For example, average prices of new semi-detached houses varied between £20,974 in the North and £27,255 in the South-East. Thus, someone selling a house in a depressed region and attempting to buy one in a prosperous region is likely to face much higher house prices in the latter, and the capital costs of trying to move may be a serious disincentive.

On the face of it, this problem should not affect local author- ity tenants. However, there are other constraints on their mobil- ity. As the last chapter showed, there are eligibility criteria for access to council housing which new migrants are unlikely to be able to meet. The main method by which council tenants move is through exchanges with other tenants. These are likely to be very difficult if one is attempting to move from a depressed area to a prosperous one. The problem is reflected in the 'Industrial Selection Schemes' and other methods for providing nominated or key workers with council housing operated by new and expanded towns. If council tenants are not 'key workers', their chances of moving to some areas are very limited.

Thus there are problems for both owner-occupiers and council tenants in moving. Evidence suggests that these problems are more likely to affect council tenants, and this group has a lower propensity to migrate long distances. While there are complex reasons for these differences, the structure of the local authority housing system itself is an important barrier to mobility.

Thus, for the bulk of potential migrants access to improved job opportunities is inextricably linked with problems over access to housing. Labour market constraints interact with those of the housing market, but again they are socially distributed – professional and managerial groups possess the material resources and social networks which facilitate mobility while manual workers not only lack such means but encounter a variety of obstacles which restrict their opportunities.

Labour markets as constraining systems

Selling one's labour power to an employer entails more than occupational rewards and disadvantages, because it occurs within an urban system. Life-chances are determined not merely by position in the labour market, but also by position in the housing market, access to environmental amenities and public services, and the range of material and intangible resources that are contained within a given area. However, it is largely *through* the labour market that workers are differentially placed *vis-à-vis* these urban resources and facilities. Thus the local industrial structure not only directly affects economic and social well-being, but sets limits on the *capacity* of individuals to modify their position within it and to move outside of it.

Economic growth and decline have enormous impacts on the

physical and social structure of areas, since industrialisation and urbanisation are inter-dependent. When markets, demand and trade fall away, or technology changes, or when companies 'rationalise' their investments by plant closures, then whole labour markets are fundamentally altered. Small amounts of 'surplus labour' can usually be reabsorbed, but major redundancies (e.g. the closure of steel works at Shotton, Port Talbot, Corby and Consett) can totally dislocate the local economy and labour market. The effects of this can be seen in the unemployment rates. For example, in 1981 unemployment in Consett was over 25 percent. Some communities, as well as being encapsulated within one industry (or by a few firms) in periods of economic growth, become trapped in an obsolete or 'fossilised' labour market in a recession. Generations of families of workers in a locality will have only experienced the particular kind of work offered there by maybe one or two firms. The workers possess homogeneous skills (or lack of skills), and alternative employment is not available – their experience, attitudes, resources and life-chances are *dominated* by the local labour market. In some respects, labour markets may be conceived of as prisons or *total institutions*, partially isolated from general conditions and operating according to their own rules.

Goffman (1968) observed that a major characteristic of total institutions is their encompassing character – all aspects of life are conducted in the same place and experienced uniformly by large numbers of similar people, often in accordance with rigid or routine schedules imposed by a superordinate system of rules and/or officials. This certainly seems to be an appropriate description of some urban labour markets.

For example, Martin and Fryer's (1973) study of a major redundancy in a town dominated by one manufacturing firm demonstrated that very few of the manual workers moved in search of jobs elsewhere. Their immobility was explained not just by their commitment to local kin and friends, and housing problems, but also because the workers held 'traditional' attitudes of deference towards their employers and accepted their unemployment as inevitable.

Thus, manual workers' practical knowledge of labour market conditions serves to limit their aspiration and creates a taken-forgrantedness, or passive resignation to economic circumstances, rather than stimulating them as active 'rational' competitors in the free market for labour.

Many workers are *trapped* in a local economy because alternative employment opportunities are not realistically available. Such situations are often characterised by an 'unbalanced' industrial base or homogeneous occupational structure, and a restricted range of worker-skills – ripe conditions for employer paternalism and/or worker dependence and deference.

Labour markets are also constraining in that they are inherently unstable, unpredictable and uncertain, particularly for manual occupations. Norris's (1978b) analysis of unemployment in Sunderland and Greenwich reveals that the chances of losing a job are disproportionately concentrated in the 'secondary' sector of the labour market. Personal characteristics of workers were found to be less important than the inherent insecurity of certain jobs in explaining unemployment. This insecurity was seen to be a normal feature of 'secondary' occupations in a dual labour market.

Blackburn and Mann's (1979) detailed study of the position of the working class in the Peterborough labour market further supports this approach. They too have observed that employment unpredictability and uncertainty are permanent problems for manual workers, together with a very limited amount of job-choice. Blackburn and Mann argue that there is very little real choice open to manual workers because jobs are similar between firms (and even between industries) and there is often little skill involved. They showed that, for almost all the workers in their sample, they used less skill at work than they would driving a car to work. Moreover, because there are numerous constraints on transfers within a labour market, workers' subjective response, according to Blackburn and Mann, is to internalise these constraints and regard them as inevitable parts of reality: they accept their market situation as given because this is how it is experienced. This experience is in contrast to that of most senior non-manual, professional and managerial occupations, where job security, high and rising incomes, and promotion ladders (involving career and geographical mobility) present a fundamentally different set of options and life-chances, and a correspondingly superior degree of choice in both labour and housing markets. Although economic recession now threatens even traditional middle class security, the relative vulnerability of the working class remains constant.

The urban and regional system and the restructuring of capital

Previous sections showed how access to jobs is not uniform, and also the uneven impact of economic change on different social groups and urban areas. We need to consider this more broadly.

'Regional problems' and 'inner city problems' are manifestations of one basic process: uneven economic development. Traditionally academic and lay perceptions tended to localise and individualise such problems, 'blaming' the areas and individuals for their 'own' shortcomings and weaknesses. Now, however, attention is increasingly directed to the structural factors responsible for economic and urban change.

Massey's (1979) analysis of the regional problem begins from the observation that at any given period there is spatial differentiation in the distribution of scarce resources. She then argues that the productive economic system responds to this in its investment, so magnifying existing inequalities. Different phases of expansion and contraction in the economy produce specialisation by type or sector of industry within certain regions, resulting in the so-called 'regional problem'. However, with falling profits and technological change – especially the growth of large conglomerate companies, and fragmentation of industrial processes and functions – it becomes necessary to adjust the pattern of capital investment. This is termed the 'restructuring of capital' and involves regional differentiation as an essential element in industrial location decisions and investment.

This takes two forms. Firstly, companies may 'rationalise' activity (as a consequence of mergers, take-overs or asset-stripping) and shut down factories or re-locate certain functions, resulting in labour redundancy. Secondly, firms create a spatial hierarchy of functions, in which, for example, mass production of components takes place in areas of unskilled, low-paid labour; assembly or new processes in areas with skilled highly-paid labour; and management and research based in prosperous small towns and cities.

The spatial restructuring of capital thus entails the development of some local economies and the desertion of others. Both inner cities and depressed regions represent in acute form the effects of this process. Evidence from the Community Development Projects (CDPs) set up by the government in twelve depressed inner city areas supports Massey's argument. The CDP teams argued that industrial decline in the inner cities was a product of structural shifts in the economy leading to local disinvestment: traditional firms collapsed, jobs disappeared, while new factories were established in greenfield sites outside the cities. Chronic and high unemployment levels were but one part of a complex nexus of factors comprising physical-environmental obsolescence, inadequate housing infrastructure and services, low incomes and a host of other indicators of 'social malaise'.

Again, however, CDP writers emphasised that industrial decline and urban deprivation were not exceptional but *normal* and even vital elements in the operation of advanced capitalist economies.

The political economy of urban change

This chapter has stressed the variation between the labour markets of different areas. These variations have effects on all aspects of the areas concerned. The features of the two extreme cases of economic contraction and economic growth shown in Table 5.1 illustrate this. It is important to recognise that these two outcomes are the result of the operation of a single process – the spatial pattern of capital investment – and that this is outside the control of the local community. It depends on the decisions of large corporations, both national and international, of central government and nationalised industries, and on international economic trends, in interest rates, and in the patterns of trade.

These two scenarios outlined are extreme cases, but they illustrate the *interaction* of economic (employment) and physical (housing) elements in the urban system. It is clear that there will be major social and political implications of the inequalities of real income implied by these trends. Different groups have diffe-

TABLE 5.1

Economic contraction/Urban decline	Economic growth/Urban development
1. Capital restructuring or rationalisation produces plant closures, obsolete factories, etc. with redundant pool of labour.	1. Growth of services and high-technology sectors of the economy; concentration of investment in high-amenity and semi-rural areas.
2. High unemployment levels, affecting particularly the young, the old and the unskilled; surplus labour with unwanted skills unable or unwilling to move to new labour and housing markets. Low incomes, poverty, dependence on state benefits and welfare services; difficulty in paying rents, mortgages, or maintaining property; high transport costs if long journeys to new jobs.	2. Recruitment of skilled, well-paid, educated workforce; expansion of senior non-manual, professional and managerial groups.
3. Loss of rate revenue to local authority, but deteriorating built environment and increased social needs puts pressure on limited resources.	3. Increased private and public investment in physical infrastructure and built environment; improved local authority rate base.
4. Negative economic multiplier effects; falling demand for goods and services; falling house prices and low demand; increased competition for council housing but inadequate provision.	4. Positive economic multiplier effects with high demand for consumer goods and services; competitive private housing market; growth of demand for amenities and facilities.
5. Labelling of area as 'problem area' or 'depressed region' acts as disincentive to investment; out-migration of younger, economically active, skilled and educated workforce; residual group of low-income, old, unskilled and dependent groups; some in-migration of marginal groups (ethnic minorities) into transient urban areas and subordinate occupations.	5. Growth of commercial development, with rising property prices, office and shop development; urban renewal/redevelopment and/or housebuilding pressure on undeveloped land.

rent *capacities* to react and respond to externally imposed change in the local economy. Some groups (or areas) are very vulnerable to economic and physical change, whereas other groups (and areas) can adapt, adjust and benefit from such change. This inequality is manifested in their unequal access to housing, employment and other opportunities.

So we see that local labour markets are important elements in the structure and processes of urban life. If we now consider the argument of Chapters 4 and 5 together, we can also see that access to work and to shelter are distinctively structured and intermeshed. However, whilst housing in the urban system is open to substantial change by the action of the local council, the job market is not so readily controlled at this level. There are a variety of political responses in this situation. Some groups may respond by voting with their feet and leaving the areas. They may even use national trade unions and professional associations to facilitate such mobility; for example, by ensuring that removal expenses are provided. Opportunities to use these strategies are necessarily limited to certain sections of the population. Some groups may respond through political pressure at the national level, for investment in an area. Other groups regard the problem as local, but within this there are a variety of forms of labour response. Different areas have characteristic styles of response which have developed over long periods of time. These range from the deference and acceptance found among Suffolk agricultural workers to the militancy of the Liverpool dockers and industrial workers.

6

THE FORMAL URBAN SYSTEM

Introduction

Local housing and labour markets, as we have seen, are not sole-ly private sector or market institutions; they are inextricably bound up with the public sector. The urban and regional sys-tem, particularly the land and property market, is subject to state intervention which facilitates and controls the distribution of resources and activities. At a subjective level, urban life is in-creasingly experienced as ,a series of encounters with complex public organisations.

By 'the formal urban system' we mean those agencies in-volved in the production, supply, administration, management and regulation of public goods and services for collective con-sumption. Those goods and services range from land, roads, sewers, water, electricity, gas, etc., through the planning sys-tem, police and fire services, to health care, education, housing and social welfare. Clearly these collective consumption facilities and resources are controlled by a *variety* of state bodies – local authorities, central government departments, nationalised indus-tries, QUANGOs (quasi-autonomous national governmental organisations, such as Regional Health Authorities, Regional Water Authorities, etc.), and so on. But the crucial point is that their role is distinctive and separate from private sector insti-tutions; their interventions are significant determinants of urban life-chances. However, although the same institutions operate universally throughout the country to carry out these functions, there are important territorial inequalities in service provision. There are widespread variations in the quality, quantity and type of urban public goods between different local authorities. Therefore, where you live determines not only your job and housing opportunities, but also the conditions of access to a whole range of services and facilities. The impact of the formal urban system is thus pervasive and substantial.

We will now briefly outline the main elements of the formal urban system. This will show not only the range of organisations involved but also the number of points at which people come into contact with it. These distinctive elements, whilst described separately below, have an overall cumulative impact. This schematic outline is not, of course, a comprehensive description of all state provision and intervention. However, the approach here is to emphasize how the range and scale of this provision contributes to the structures and processes of urban life. For example, the interaction between the personal social services and participation in the labour market of, for example, women is not always recognised in conventional accounts.

1 *Urban development* is still primarily 'driven' by private market forces, and the state is only involved through the *regulation* and negative control of land use by the planning system. Roads and other infrastructures are, however, largely provided by state agencies.

2 *The housing market* involves a variety of interventions by the state, as we have shown in Chapter 4.

3 *The National Health Service* provides a whole range of services in addition to general practice provision, clinics and hospitals. But even in the case of GPs, there is wide variation in the number of people on doctors' lists, so that in practice, doctors in some areas can be seen more readily than in others. In spite of attempts to reorganise and to streamline the system, there are persistent regional and social class variations in ill health and in the amount and standards of medical care (see Townsend and Davidson 1982).

4 *The personal social services* run by local government are meant to provide support and a variety of services for people who cannot or do not fully participate in economic and social life. Thus some of the old, the sick and the young are partially catered for, and the welfare state to that extent removes the burden of care from the family (i.e. women), allowing women in particular to participate in the labour market. With rising levels

of unemployment, there has been a shift away from this kind of policy towards more 'care in the community' – this means in practice, care by women again.

5 *The social security system* is nationally organised but locally administered and makes cash payments to alleviate poverty caused by unemployment, disability or sickness. At the end of 1978, nearly 3 million people were receiving 'supplementary benefit' – 59 percent of these were pensioners and 20 percent were unemployed. However, there are numerous groups excluded from eligibility for these benefits, and those that are eligible face means-tests, a bewildering set of regulations (illustrated in the past in the Supplementary Benefits Commission's Handbook, 1977), and often hostile bureaucratic gatekeepers. The system has been criticised because it stigmatises claimants, discriminates against women and relies heavily upon discretionary decisions by officials.

6 *The educational system* historically grew up to supply the needs of the labour market for trained workers, even though in practice it did not always seem to be doing that, and now, with a contracting labour market, the state is more reluctant to support the system: teacher training colleges and schools have been closed and this retrenchment may continue. Educational success does vary throughout the country and councils differ in the kind of school system (selective or comprehensive) provided, as well as in the investment of resources. For example, there are marked variations in expenditures on facilities such as careers services. In the years 1979–80, the average expenditure was £317,000, but Kent spent £1,065,000, while Hampshire had no separate careers service at all.

7 *Employment services* are almost completely controlled now by a state agency with local offices. Since 1973, the Manpower Services Commission has worked to improve the efficiency of local labour markets by providing assistance for people to select, train for, obtain and retain suitable employment. With rising unemployment, these functions have become more politically sensitive. Throughout the country, local offices and 'Job Centres' attempt to match job vacancies with potential workers; provide advice and career guidance; make training facilities, grants and transfers available, etc. In 1978–79, the MSC spent over

£500 million – £57 million was grant aid for the 'Youth Opportunities Programme' and £8.5 million was for the 'Special Temporary Employment Programme'. The former scheme provided unemployed school leavers with some training and work experience, while the latter provided younger unemployed adults with temporary jobs. The total number involved in MSC programmes has risen from nil in 1975 to over 300,000 in 1977, and over 700,000 at the end of 1980, though not all of these involve full-time jobs. Although these measures are small in scale when measured against rising unemployment, they represent growing state intervention in the labour market and the incorporation of employment as an element of social welfare.

Thus the formal urban system consists of a multiplicity of essentially bureaucratic state institutions whose activities influence the distribution of opportunities and resources in many aspects of people's lives. The administration of the welfare services is largely controlled by officials who often exercise discretionary powers. However, the exercise of these powers reflects political decisions by local authorities. In particular, attitudes to spending are politically structured and over long periods of time authorities develop characteristic approaches to spending. Some regard keeping down expenditure as their main objective, while others are prepared to spend more freely. Other authorities may vary over time with change of political control. Political discretion may be seen in other areas of policy. The differing policies of local authorities to the implementation of comprehensive education is a particularly striking example. As a result, there are social and spatial inequalities in access to the resources they provide.

The formal urban system is characterised by complexity, heterogeneity and fragmentation. These features were identified as the causes of confusion, uncertainty and ambiguity in central/ local relationships in recent government reports and have become the object of a major research programme. The implementation of policies is regarded as problematic because of difficult inter-governmental relations and variation caused by local autonomy. Moreover, the allocation of urban resources must be seen not only in the context of interlocking and overlapping state bureaucracies, but also in the context of interactions between the state and the private sectors.

Several writers have used the term 'local state' to refer to these institutions and to emphasise the close relationship they have with the central government in a welfare state. However, this concept also implies the necessity of seeing local councils and other local institutions as more than mere agencies of the central state. They are components of a state which perform a societal role, creating conditions for the operation and maintenance of the economic and political system. There have been disagreements in the discussion of the local state about the extent to which it performs a role which is autonomous from the central state, and thus how far local agencies can be independent actors. In the years ahead this is likely to be more than just a matter of academic debate, but a central question about the future and operation of the welfare state.

Growth of the local state, 1960–1980

The elements of the formal urban system outlined above have grown in importance very rapidly over the last thirty years, and this may be seen in the rapid growth of expenditure on welfare and related services and the growth of employment in local government.

Public expenditure generally has risen steadily as a proportion of national income and output from the mid-1960s, rising from about 42 percent of Gross Domestic Product in 1961 to 58 percent of GDP in 1975. It has subsequently declined as successive governments have attempted to reduce state spending with freezes, cash-limits and cuts. These figures include all forms of public expenditure, including those of nationalised industries, but a major component of the growth in spending has been on welfare state or 'social' services – education, health, personal social services, social security and housing, much of which is consumed locally and administered by local authorities. The 1960s especially were a period of rapid growth in welfare expenditure, with its share of GNP rising from 18 percent in 1961 to 29 percent by 1975. The major increases were in health and personal social services, and state education. As we shall see below, this growth in expenditure has given rise to considerable strains on the formal urban system, particularly in local government.

Manpower

As with the growth of public expenditure generally, the expansion of public sector manpower was a response to economic and social change, legislation and rising needs, demands and expectations in the welfare state. There was a 1½ million increase in the number of employees in the public sector (i.e. central and local governments and public corporations) between 1961 and 1978, reaching a total of 7.4 million workers in 1978. Within this total, local authority employment grew from 1.8 million to 3 million. The mid-1960s and early 1970s were periods of rapid growth in public sector manpower generally, and the number of staff working for local authority education and social services departments, and National Health Service employees, almost *doubled* in the period 1961–78 (even after accounting for changes due to re-organisation), and they together represented over 40 percent of all public sector employees in 1978.

TABLE 6.1   *Local authority manpower by service, 1979 (England and Wales)*

Service	Percentage
Education	48
Construction	6
Transport	1
Social Services	10
Libraries and Museums	2
Recreation and Parks	4
Environmental Health	1
Refuse Collection and Disposal	2
Housing	2
Town and Country Planning	1
Fire Service	2
Police	7
Probation and Magistrates' Courts	0.8
Miscellaneous Services	13
Total numbers	2,090,769

Source: *Employment Gazette*, May 1980, p. 510

Table 6.1 shows the manpower in the range of services local authorities perform. Local authorities employ different categories of employees: some are professional and technical staff, some administrative, and many are clerical and manual workers. Each service has a different ratio of these categories, and this has significance for the level of unionisation and the degree of social power exercised by these groups, as we shall see in the final section of this chapter.

The reorganisation of the local state

In parallel with this growth of local state, there has been substantial reorganisation of the various agencies involved. We cannot offer a detailed discussion here of all these changes, but we can outline important developments. The pressure for this reorganisation stemmed from changes in the national and local patterns of employment, population growth, transport and the demand for housing and urban development, but there were also longstanding arguments about the scope of local government activities, the distribution of functions between levels of government and local government boundaries. Through the 1960s and 1970s there were a variety of Royal Commissions, inquiries, research and official reports on virtually every aspect of urban administration, service delivery, decision-making and finance. These reports reflected an attempt to apply the 'managerial revolution' in local government, and several 'orthodoxies', as Dearlove (1979) labelled them, came to dominate the debate: the search for efficiency and rationality, the need for co-ordination both within and between agencies; improvement in officer and councillor calibre; and the desire to strengthen local accountability and democracy. Evidence on the inequalities of service provision between areas added to the arguments for reform.

In local government, there was a reorganisation of London government in 1963, and for the rest of England and Wales in 1974 and Scotland in 1975. These set up a two-tier division of functions between counties and districts (regions and districts in Scotland). The districts generally controlled housing and local planning and environmental services, while the counties controlled education, social services, transport, police and structure planning. (In the conurbations there was a different distribution of functions, with education and social services controlled by the districts.)

Reaction to these changes has been mixed, and there have been numerous examples of inter-authority disputes about policies across the range of services. Party political differences (often reflecting urban versus suburban and rural interests) have ensured that county/district relationships are precarious, especially over what constitutes 'strategic' versus 'local' matters.

Local authorities purport to be institutions which allow local populations to manage their own environment and decide their own level of services. However, the expansion of the welfare state has made it impossible for local authorities to raise sufficient revenue from local taxation. As a result, about 60 percent of local government expenditure is met by central government in the form of the Rate Support Grant. Moreover, central government has always been concerned that local government should be cost-effective and under the financial control of Whitehall, in order to conform with national economic objectives.

These factors have a number of important implications. In the first place, the criteria on which the Rate Support Grant is determined have important effects in benefiting different types of areas. The formula used to calculate the grant has two main elements: a needs element, based on the characteristics of the population the local authority is serving; and a resources element, related to the authority's rate base The formula itself is an enormously complicated computer program. The technical rationality that this implies is misleading. The details of the formulae involve political choices about which areas should benefit. At different times, the system has benefited inner city areas with a declining rate base and acute social problems, or rural areas with growing populations and growing needs for services. The system is thus the object of considerable political conflict. Secondly, the extent of central finance of local authorities gives the government considerable scope for determining objectives. This is exacerbated by recent public expenditure reductions, and in 1980 central government took powers to set spending limits for individual authorities, and penalise those which over-stepped them. These factors mean that the ability of local populations to set their own priorities is substantially reduced.

Fiscal crisis of the local state

The problem of financing local government is an integral part of the general problem of financing the welfare state, or the 'social wage'. The social wage refers to all those benefits and services in cash or kind provided by the state over and above private wages or income. Some writers argue that the provision of the social wage is essential in order to maintain the economic and social fabric of a capitalist society. However, the costs of the welfare state tend to rise and become potentially threatening to private sector profitability.

O'Connor (1973), for example, asserts that the state must perform two essential but often conflicting functions – supporting the process of capital accumulation and profits, and legitimating capitalism's economic, social and political structure. Public expenditure is thus necessary, he says, to increase labour productivity, minimise the costs of reproducing labour power and to maintain social and political integration. However, these expenditures tend to deplete private sector profits and constitute an increasing burden, giving rise to a 'fiscal crisis' for the state.

In addition to being an economic problem, the fiscal crisis also constitutes a *political* problem because of the conflict of interest between 'productive' spending, which directly assists capital, and 'non-productive' spending, which goes to support the working population. Political pressure for increased provision of housing, hospitals, schools, etc. by the local (and national) state may result in the expansion of public spending, but, as we have already observed, inflation and recession accelerate the fiscal crisis and lead to greater intervention by central government to minimise local government budgets.

Economic crisis results in a paradoxical situation: rising unemployment, poverty, urban deprivation and housing problems all create extra demands for welfare and local authority services, but public expenditure cuts diminish the size of the social wage. Gough (1979) reports that two further developments are then likely: first, state intervention becomes more explicitly geared to the needs of the productive private sector economy; and, second, the need to contain and ameliorate social problems and political protest requires greater investment in agencies of social control, such as the police.

Thus, the provision of the social wage and the management of the urban system by the local state are fundamental to the operation of the labour market and economy. Intervention in 'manpower planning', tightening controls over the social security system, moral panics over 'welfare scroungers', anxiety about the 'relevance' of education, and coercive aspects of social work, can all be interpreted as part of the state's overriding preoccupation with the need for a viable (but docile) labour force and an efficient economy. Other local government and state welfare services (housing, health, transport, planning) have similar effects. We return to these questions in Chapter 8.

There is evidently a close connection between the formal urban system and the labour market, and since each operates as a determinant of life-chances it is essential that we analyse the bureaucracies involved. Given that 'social wage' allocation is not primarily governed by market criteria (at least in principle), but by bureaucratically-defined criteria of need (resting upon administrative case-law and practice), we should examine the role, influence and interests of those who manage the urban system.

Urban managers and the 'social wage salariat'

The recognition that inequalities in the urban system derive largely from variations in the allocation of scarce goods and services was the basis of Pahl's (1975) argument that certain groups of 'urban managers' are important and powerful decision-makers in the social and spatial structure. The emphasis was on the fact that these gatekeepers or managers determined the eligibility of consumers or clients, assessed their needs, and made allocation decisions which could reduce or increase existing social inequalities resulting from a household's position in the labour market. In other words, urban managers exercise some *independent* influence on life-chances, and, if this was so, it is important to examine their ideologies, action and degree of power.

This idea stimulated considerable discussion and criticism. The main difficulties with the concept of urban managers centred on its relevance for both public and private sectors, problems of identifying the managers empirically, and, most important, assessing the extent of managers' influence in the context of structural constraints on their autonomy. These problems are substantial, but the question of the actual or potential *mediating* role played by state bureaucrats in the distribution of the social wage remains important.

Earlier we documented the growth of personnel in the formal urban system. We argued that the welfare state and formal urban system have created a new professional and semi-professional group of state employees which can be termed the 'social wage salariat'. In principle, their work is rational, bureaucratic or technical rather than being determined by profit or market considerations (although their functions may be supportive of the private sector).

In effect, the social wage salariat constitutes a distinct social stratum, but its social location is ambiguous. Johnson (1972) has described the development of quasi-professional groupings created by 'state mediation'. Here the state defines the relationship between a 'professional' producer and a consumer or client, and the state determines the nature of clients' needs and the content of service provided. Such a process seems evident in the formal urban system, since state-professionals (or urban managers) play significant roles in health, education, etc. Johnson (1977) claims that:

occupational definitions of, for example, success and failure in education, sickness, and health, and normal behaviour, are subordinated to or derived from 'official' definitions . . .

This analysis seems appropriate in the interpretation of the services described above – planning, housing, health, social security, education, etc. And it raises again the question: 'Whose interests are served – the officials', the clients', the state's?'

Professionalisation and bureaucratisation of local government officials have undoubtedly led to the emergence of powerful public sector interest groups. Two processes have been at work: first, attempts by officers to establish their technical expertise and 'professional' standards of service; second, the growth of white-collar unionisation to further occupational rewards and security of council staff. Within local authorities the functional departments have increasingly employed workers with higher educational and professional qualifications, and this has contributed to changing patterns of service. Trades union membership has also tended to increase demands for greater finance to extend and improve the *services* as well as to enhance pay and defend jobs.

Health, education and other local government employees are highly unionised, and although many of these are manual workers (for example, the National Union of Public Employees has over 700,000 members), white collar workers are very important, and their union, the National and Local Government Officers Association, has over 720,000 members.

Thus, there are over half a million teachers, over 21,000 social workers, more than 21,000 staff in town and country planning, over 48,000 in housing departments, and more than 20,000 involved in transport in English local authorities. Individually and collectively, these officials are engaged in delivering resources and managing the environment under the variable control of local councillors and in accordance with a variety of rationales.

Several issues arise from the role of the social wage salariat. First, there is the question of how some encounters between officials and claimants or clients have a repressive or coercive character: labelling and stigma are inevitably part of such hierarchical interactions, when the consumer is effectively a supplicant. Second, there is the empirical question of how far officials and bureaucrats pre-empt the policy agendas and decisions of politicians – the extent of bureaucratic power and autonomy. Third, how far does the social wage salariat pursue its own special occupational or professional interests? There is evidence, for example, that the medical profession has considerable influence on the structure and policies of the NHS. Social work's occupational ambiguity and its claim for professional status also has effects on social work practices. Similarly, other bodies (like the Royal Town Planning Institute, Royal Institute of British Architects, Institute of Housing Managers, etc.) function as staff unions *and* as lobby groups in discussions of legislation and practice. Fourth, the relationship of urban managers to central government and to the private sector is fundamental in the formation and implementation of urban policies. Senior council officials regularly interact with government departments, industrial and commercial companies, financial institutions, etc., as well as local interest groups and politicians. They therefore function as filters or mediators between central and local government, and between the private and public sector of the urban distributive system.

Conclusion: the management of everyday life

This chapter has shown how the formal urban system occupies a strategic position in the structure and processes of urban life. The last twenty years have witnessed dramatic changes in the character and scope of state intervention. There have been major changes in the institutional arrangements of local government and the welfare state, and in the importance of the social wage. Local government especially has undergone rapid expansion in budgets and personnel, but has encountered severe financial and political problems.

Despite apparent fragmentation, a common concern in the formal urban system is the allocation of the social wage, socially and spatially. Economic crisis has generated fiscal and political contradictions in the provision of collective consumption, as increased social demands are met by decreased public expenditure. In this context, the role of the social wage salariat (or urban managers), although constrained by structural factors, is undoubtedly important.

The state now dominates households and penetrates private life. Indeed, the *pervasiveness* of state intervention is now probably so great that it has become taken for granted, precisely because it does affect so many aspects of urban life. From the mundane matters of the route, times and cost of local buses to the closure of a hospital or school, individual households experience the effects of bureaucratic and political decisions about resource allocation. Arguably, just about every facet of ordinary domestic life involves the state in one form or another – the availability of council housing, refuse collection, building and planning regulations, unemployment benefits, and so on. Positive aspects of service provision are accompanied by negative aspects of exclusion and regulation: thus permission can be refused, benefits or grants withheld, children can be removed from a family and put into 'care', and so on.

Castells (1977) has argued that the scale and pace of state intervention in welfare-capitalist societies is now so great that it has *politicised* the urban scene in a new way. The organisation and management of the means of collective consumption – including housing, schools, transport, health facilities, welfare services and urban planning – is so dominated by the formal urban system that, for Castells, the state has become 'the real manager of everyday life'. One effect of this is the emergence of community-based protest groups, but these are usually concerned with localised specific issues, rather than with any generalised 'urban politics'. Castells' approach is discussed in detail by Saunders (1981).

Much of this analysis of state power was developed in a period of economic growth, but the argument is just as applicable in a period of recession. Massive unemployment, growing dependency on social security and other welfare benefits, and sustained demand for urban resources undoubtedly increase pressure on the state, whose capacity to respond is limited by economic crisis. More claims on the social wage, and thus even scarcer resources, entails further regulation and restrictions on eligibility, so strengthening the gatekeeping role of those who allocate those resources.

With the institutionalisation of complex allocation rules and procedures in state bureaucracies, so there emerges a structure of accessibility in which households and local populations are differently located. This social structure influencing urban life-chances is compounded by territorial inequalities in allocation and accessibility. Thus, similar households with similar occupations and wages may have different real incomes and life-chances. They may encounter quite different treatment by officials in different local offices of the same council department or ministry, and they may enjoy or suffer quite different levels of service provision in different parts of the country.

This chapter has demonstrated the growth in scale and range of functions of the local state and the social wage salariat. There remains an important issue of who has gained from this growth.

It appears, paradoxically, that while the local state has grown in scale, this has not led to an increase in local power to counterbalance the centre. Rather, it would appear that it is the power of the central state which has grown. This issue of power has always been one of the central questions in the sociological analysis of 'the urban'. It is pursued further in Chapter 8.

7

WORK OUTSIDE EMPLOYMENT

Inevitably, the last three chapters have focussed on the institutionally structured processes determining urban life in contemporary British cities. However, in practice, of course, people's lives are not so directly determined: systems operate less rigidly and there are more cracks and crevices in the structures in which people may gain and exercise autonomy. Conversely, even the so-called informal work of everyday domestic life is more structured through the physical separation of home and work and the overall subordinate position of women. The intermeshing of the formal and the informal is one of the main themes of this chapter.

The changing nature of work

Work in urban industrial society is typically seen as something one 'goes to'. One returns home 'after work', but it is evident that much other work is done in and around the home. The work of caring for children, cooking, cleaning and washing and repairing clothes has come to be seen as specifically women's work, since work which could be industrialised was taken out of the home into the factories and mines of early industrial England. The notion that 'women's place is in the home', doing specific tasks known as housework, is thus a relatively recent idea. In *The Boke of Husbandry* by Anthony Fitzherbert, published in 1568 as a guide to estate management, we are told

It is a wyves occupation to wynowe all maner of cornes . . . to make heye, shere corn, and in tyme of nede to helpe her husbande to fyll the muck-wayne or dounge-cart, dryve the ploughe, to loode heye, corne and such other.

She would certainly have a whole range of other tasks to do as well and there might be a sharp division of labour between the man and his wife. However, the relegation of women to a state of permanent dependency on 'the breadwinner' is a product of nineteenth-century industrial urbanism.

The emergence of a separate social category, 'the housewife', was paralleled by a physical separation of home and work which reinforced her social dependency. Before the end of the eighteenth century, there was a much less marked social and physical segregation between the spheres of men and women between types of work. Autobiographies of Cornish miners in the eighteenth century describe how they kept smallholdings and worked on them between time in the mines with the other members of their families. Much of the woollen industry was run on the putting-out system, where all members of the household worked as part of a family productive unit. It was not possible to make sharp distinctions in the eighteenth century between agriculture and manufacture or mining, and the dichotomy of town/industry as opposed to village/agriculture was hardly applicable. As commerce, business and manufacture expanded, it was still common in the late eighteenth century for the factory owner to live adjoining the works, or the banker to carry on his business in the front room of his house. Work of men, women and children, although different, would be visible to each other and different tasks and types of work would not be segregated spatially. To take a seemingly trivial example, not only would all members of the family eat all meals together, but any break for refreshment might bring husband and wife together, perhaps to entertain a customer or perhaps just to exchange talk on how various tasks of the day were progressing.

The separation of home and work

The expansion of urban industrial society in the nineteenth century segregated the social and economic spheres of men and women and forced apart the different kinds of work done by members of the household. Vast areas of workers' housing were built, first around the factories and later further away as developments in transport and cheap fares encouraged the development of commuting. The physical separation of home and work was even greater for the middle class. New suburbs focussed on the railway stations of the expanding system like beads on a chain. New residential developments were advertised, emphasising the healthiness of bringing up families away from the noise, dirt and pollution of the manufacturing cities.

When, in the twentieth century, Town Planning developed as a separate profession, this segregation of residential areas from centres of employment became an established tenet. So, even when industry created very little noise, dirt or disturbance or, in the case of offices, nothing but some extra traffic, it was still kept far away from women and children. This, of course, severely limited women's prospects for getting paid employment, particularly for part-time work which might fit in better with the other work that had to be done.

This physical separation of spheres is so much taken for granted that its consequences have only recently been questioned. Women and the family were, in a sense, taken out of the economy and the home became less a centre of production and more a centre of reproduction of the labour force. Men then retreated from the public world of work to the private world of the home where they could recuperate and prepare themselves for their next day's labour. The multiplication of each little family in a home of its own meant that there was a vast market for consumer goods. Arguably, much of economic growth of the 1950s and 1960s was based on the expansion of the market for cars, washing machines and other such consumer durables. The effect of every household having its own car, TV set or washing machine meant that the use of public transport, cinemas and laundries declined. Goods and services which had been supplied and consumed publicly came to be consumed privately in the home. The growth of separate residential areas thus came to be seen as reinforcing women's dependency on men and limiting their prospects for employment and as the foundation of a privatised consumerism, which helped to fuel the growth and expansion of the capitalist economy. So parts of cities are concerned with production and other parts are concerned with reproduction. For children, the world of work is taken away from their everyday experience and becomes, rather, something that they enter at some later period of their lives. Schools, which are also, typically, sited away from centres of employment, have to prepare youngsters for something that seems remote and curiously unreal.

Urban working class children used to have far more opportunity to engage in all kinds of work than they do now. Research by oral historians has documented the host of informal jobs that most urban children did, often when they were still at school. Milk rounds, paper rounds, window washing, errand running, baby minding, carrying luggage, opening cab doors and so forth all provided money and helped to provide first-hand knowledge and experience of urban life.

In his book on *The Edwardians*, based largely on the memories of those he interviewed, Paul Thompson (1977) provides fascinating detail on urban life in the early twentiety century. He reports one lad who would

hang about on the platform, and wait till the cabs are loaded up with luggage, then you'd sit behind and ride to where the cab stopped, see? And then you'd help the driver unpack the baggage and carry it in, he'd give you threepence, yes. And you do that two or three times a night and you'd had a good night, you'd have a fish supper and all for two pence.

Very often such activities depended entirely on the individual's initiative and there was no boss to set the pace. We are not saying that many youngsters don't do such work now – whether or not they play truant to do so; it is simply that there were many more opportunities for such informal work in Edwardian England than there are now and there were fewer legal constrictions. We are also emphasising that in new council estates or in leafy middle class suburbs, there is much less scope for doing work of this kind. This should be considered beside Colin Ward's suggestion in his vivid book, *The Child in the City* (1977):

in the ideal city every school would be a productive workshop and every workshop an effective school.

Continuities and discontinuities in informal work

In pre-industrial England there were many ancient rights which allowed people access to fuel, timber and tools to repair their homes, and pasture on which they could graze their animals. These benefits in kind were gradually reduced by such measures as Acts of Enclosure, and what had once been customary practice became defined as a crime. The gradual translation of 'rights' (held in common) into 'property', or 'capital' (held in particular) was going on as a new urban working class was being created. Some of the rural styles and expectations carried over into the towns. It has been argued by one authority (Rule 1981) that much 'criminal' activity occurs in the transformation of the wage from a form in which monetary payment did not cover the whole wage to one exclusively based on money:

Bugging to the hatter, cabbage to the tailor, blue-pigeon flying to plumbers and glaziers, chippings to shipwrights, sweepings to porters, red sailyard docking to navy yard workers, fints and thrums to weavers, vails to servants, privileges to west country clothiers, bontages to Scottish agricultural workers, scrappings and naxers to coopers, wastages to framework knitters, in all these the eighteenth century labourer appropriated part of his product or a part of the materials in his labour.

Every trade or craft had its customary perquisites and the fact that there were specific colloquialisms for specific practices suggests that such activity was not seen in the same way as simply 'nicking' or 'pinching'. Embezzlement of materials by outworkers was particularly common and it has been argued that the early development of the factory system was less due to the exigencies of the technology of the expanding textile industry, but more to the capitalists' need to control the workforce. Be that as it may, different localities and different trades and occupations had their distinctive expectations about what could be customarily claimed. Workers in the Admiralty dockyards, for example, had a long-standing right to take out chips for firewood. So much timber and other materials were taken from some yards that the men were said to be building their own houses out of timber intended for the construction of ships.

Customary practices and perquisites have gradually disappeared to be replaced with more formal benefits, such as subsidised canteens, company cars and special pension schemes. However, with the reduction in the length of the working day and the ready availability of do-it-yourself tools and materials, the opportunities for productive work in and around the home have expanded enormously. Not only can people maintain and decorate their own homes in their own time, but they can use their relatively easily acquired skills to make money by doing similar work for others.

Areas will differ very greatly in the opportunity structures they offer for work outside employment. The more varied the local environment, by and large the more there will be ways of improving one's position through informal work. Houses that are owner-occupied and have got to the age when they require substantial repair and maintenance provide perhaps the best incentive to work outside employment. An unemployed person might be able to gain more by doing up and selling a house than by selling his labour for a not very substantial wage. Large, local authority-owned estates, particularly if they are high-rise, provide, perhaps, the worst kind of environment for this kind of work. Similarly, in areas which have been developed in a rather piecemeal manner, there are likely to be small workshops or structures which can be converted to other uses more readily.

Gardens and allotments are another resource which vary in their availability from one area to another. Anyone taking a train journey within and between urban areas in Britain will notice the contrast between those areas which are barren and bricked over and those areas with the patchwork quilt of allotments, with each little patch intensively cultivated and with its makeshift shed and other signs of the owner's individuality. The number of allotment holders has grown considerably in recent years. In London, the number of occupied plots has risen from 45,824 in 1967 to 53,414 in 1977; and whilst there was a considerable number of vacant plots in 1967, by 1977 there was a waiting list of 16,364. Gardening and horticulture are extremely widespread activities. The General Household Survey of 1977 reported that in the third quarter of the year, 56 per cent of those interviewed claimed to have done some gardening in the previous four weeks. The existence of private urban horticulture is frequently unnoticed, yet the yield per hectare is as high as anywhere in the world, and the work and skill involved can be substantial.

The greater the variation in the local physical environment, the more the opportunity for other kinds of work. The more the locality is officially planned and organised, very often the less scope there is to find the cracks in the urban fabric in which something productive can grow. But we are not referring simply to the physical fabric. Much depends also on the local occupational structure. There are some occupations which provide the time for other work: thus postmen and milkmen may have finished their day's work soon after midday. Similarly, dockworkers and contract labourers may get periods between bursts of employment when they are able to do other work. Some workers have skills which are more useful than others for engaging in shadow-wage work. Plumbers, electricians, car mechanics and plasterers all have scope for earning extra money or for doing favours for friends and neighbours.

In a survey of double-job workers in Cardiff, Alden (1977) has shown that 80 per cent of double-job workers' main job was in service industry and 17 per cent in the manufacturing sector. Indeed, in the Cardiff study four groups of occupations accounted for 70 per cent of second jobs – sales workers, service occupations, professional and technical workers and teachers. There are, of course, great difficulties in defining what a second job is. In Britain, data from the General Household Survey and the Family Expenditure Survey (FES) suggest 3 per cent and 7.3 per cent respectively as the rates for double-job holding in Britain in 1976. The FES data for 1976 identified female rates of 9.3 per cent, whereas the male rate was 5.9 per cent. This may be accounted for by activities such as running mail order catalogues or organising Avon or Tupperware-selling parties. The second job for females is much less likely to be one of employee status – only about a quarter – whereas for males second jobs are divided fairly evenly between those that are of employee status and those that are not. Overall, about a third of double-job holders are women. Most people do the second job to get some money, but it is significant that in Alden's Cardiff study 13 per cent of the single job holders did some form of *unpaid* work, which was more than double the rate of employed people holding paid second jobs.

Perhaps the best source of information on the work that people actually do is provided by Time Budget Studies. Gershuny and Thomas (1980) have shown that over the period from 1961 to 1974–5, the amount of time devoted to paid work has declined. More significantly, however, there has been a redistribution between the sexes, with men doing a larger proportion of the domestic work and women increasing their proportion of paid work. But, again, there are differences between social categories. Those in the top 30 per cent of the population who have access to the relatively better paid and intrinsically rewarding jobs have increased the proportion of paid work they do relative to housework, whereas the rest, who have access to the less desirable paid jobs, have shifted their distribution of work towards work in the household. The man who says 'it paid me to take two weeks off work to paint the house' expresses the shift very aptly. Hence, Gershuny and Thomas conclude with the axiom that 'the lower the relative wage and intrinsic job satisfaction, the larger the proportion of working time spent in individual production'. Gershuny has also demonstrated that between 1959 and 1977 the average family consumption of services declined. Parallel with that decline has been an increased expenditure on goods – people provide their own travel and amusement with their car and their TV set, and they fix their own shelf with a power drill rather than calling in a jobbing builder. It was this line of thinking which led Gershuny (1978) to title his first book *After Industrial Society? The Emerging Self-Service Economy*.

New concepts of work

It is evident from what has been said so far that work outside employment is an essential element in urban life and that there appears to be a shift in the proportion of time being devoted to one kind of work at the expense of another. Social anthropologists, who are, perhaps, less bound by the conventional views of work held in industrial society, see it more broadly as the production of necessary tasks and necessary values (moral as well as economic). Sandra Wallman argues that 'the task of meeting obligations, securing identity, status and structure are as fundamental to livelihood as bread and shelter'. On this basis, work may be defined as the production, management or conversion of the resources necessary to livelihood. She takes these necessary resources to be land, labour, capital, time, information and identity:

Work is then not only 'about' the production of material goods, money transactions and the need to grow food and to cook the family dinner. It must equally be 'about' the ownership and circulation of information, the playing of roles, the symbolic affirmation of personal significance and group identity – and the relation of each of these to the other. (Wallman 1979)

Other kinds of work, not in formal workplaces or in the home, are quite likely not rewarded in financial terms. People who do work for others in their locality might be offended if they were offered money. Their assumption would more likely to be that the service or favour given could be appropriately repaid in similar style at a later date. Thus, fresh vegetables from one man's allotment may be repaid some time afterwards by borrowing jump leads to start his car which has a flat battery. Women might exchange time baby-sitting for each other, and so on. Stuart Henry's study of *The Hidden Economy* (1978) unfortunately focussed almost entirely on the distribution and circulation of stolen goods, but the processes he described can equally well apply to activities which are in no way illegal. He showed that people took part in this activity very often more for social than for economic rewards. One informant, for example, preferred money to be given to the barman of his regular pub as a kind of kitty. This man then never had the need to carry money: if he wanted to have a drink or treat his friends, he knew his bank behind the bar would always be in credit.

It is often very difficult to know what kind of work a person is doing unless much more is known about the context in which it is performed. It may, therefore, be useful to introduce a way of conceptualising the work that goes on every day in our towns and cities. We must first make a distinction between work that is concerned with production and that which is concerned with re-production. Work for production is relatively easy to understand, if we see it largely in terms of work for wages or salary, either by working for an employer or for oneself. Such work is structured by market relations and it supports that other work which operates under exactly the same conditions, except that it is done informally 'for cash' and little evidence appears openly in the National Accounts. Quite a substantial amount of productive economic activity goes unrecorded in this way, but whilst the surveilling and controlling agencies of the state see this as a problem, conceptually it is hard to distinguish this work in any other way than that it is simply unrecorded.

Work for reproduction purposes poses many more difficulties. Not only must we physically reproduce ourselves – day by day and from generation to generation – but we have to reproduce the social relations of our particular kind of society or social formation. And we have to reproduce a consciousness which confirms that the social relations we have reproduced are acceptable. This is all much more complicated, and some sociologists are grappling with the difficulties and confusions that this creates. This may be illustrated by what happens when a young man and a young woman decide to live together. If they are both in paid employment, they have to decide between them how the domestic tasks are to be apportioned. Various bargains and trade-offs will be struck and, for the sake of our argument, this is done fairly and both partners accept it as such. This work that they do we may define as individual reproductive work, even though they are living together. Take, by contrast, another couple where the man assumes that on marriage his wife ceases her employment to look after him and his home. We would then define it as a form of work which reproduced the system of inequality based on patriarchy. Other types of this form of work are concerned with maintaining other hierarchies of power and privilege, such as those related to class or race. Unless we know a great deal about the social relations within which the functions of production and reproduction are performed, we cannot be sure what kind of work it is. Imagine a woman ironing a garment in her home. This activity could be any of the following kinds of work:

1 she could be completing a task for which she is employed as an outworker for a garment manufacturer (wage labour);
2 she could be completing a garment which she proposes to sell in her own stall or boutique (petty commodity production);
3 she could be completing a garment which she proposes to sell to get some extra cash which she will not declare to the state (this could be either shadow wage labour or shadow petty commodity production);
4 she could be ironing her own clothes to get herself ready for

tomorrow's work (individual reproduction);

5 she could be performing her task as a housewife solely dependent on her husband (social reproduction and/or reproduction
of patriarchal values);

6 she could be helping a neighbour by doing work which might
later be repaid by a similar service (social solidarity work);

7 she might be ironing a garment for the local dramatic society
which had been more or less imposed on her by the way the
decision was taken by stronger members of the group (reproduction of social hierarchy).

The list could be extended in many ways. The intention is simply to show that the same task, the same activity, can be either
work for production or work for reproduction, depending on the
social relations within which it is embedded. What *kind* of productive or reproductive work has also to be determined.

As we have seen, there have been shifts between one kind of
work over time and there will be considerable differences in the
mix of these different kinds of work from place to place and between households in those places. Among the broader tendencies
accounting for these shifts we may mention the restructuring of
capital and the consequent differing levels of unemployment between different industries and different labour markets, which
we discussed in Chapter 5. This may also affect the relative
balance between men and women who are formally employed.
Then there are changes in legislation which make work which
was once customary or legal become illegal. This ranges from
limiting access to common land to the introduction of Value
Added Tax and Employment Protection legislation. Much work
became illegal overnight as a result of a new piece of legislation
being passed. Another general tendency is the development of
technology which has produced the goods which enable households to produce goods and services for themselves. Also of
general importance is the raising of women's consciousness so that
they define patriarchal subordination work as demeaning. These
economic, political, legal and ideological tendencies help to produce distinctive mixes of work. At a more local level, there are
all the particular ecological and social factors which have been
mentioned. The degree of social turbulence in an area may affect
the amount of work needed for social solidarity. The people you

know and the more they know each other and see each other regularly, the greater are the obligations that may be imposed upon you. Neighbours and colleagues will ask favours and do favours for the people they know. Since increasingly it is *whom* you know rather than *what* you know, the interconnectedness of local networks becomes an important determinant of styles of work.

Conclusions

Our concern in this chapter with domestic, communal and informal work opens up a distinctive way of approaching urban life. The stereotypical view of work being what the husband does between the time he leaves his wife in the morning to when he returns in the evening has to be amended. In areas of high unemployment it may well be the woman who leaves her husband at home whilst she goes to employment, even if only on a part-time basis. It is also significant that the family of the conventional advertisements – father and mother and two children (inevitably one of each sex) – is only a small proportion of the total number of households. As Table 7.1 shows, the 'image family' comprises only a fifth of all households.

The ideas in this chapter have been discussed for a relatively short time and empirical research is sparse. Current studies funded by the Social Science Research Council will produce detailed results about work outside employment towards the end of

TABLE 7.1 *Household types (1976 General Household Survey)*

	(%)
Nuclear family with children:	
single breadwinner	20
dual worker	20
Married couple, no children	27
One parent family household	8
One parent household:	
over retirement age	15
under retirement age	6
Two or more people, not a family	3
Two or more families	1
Total	100

the 1980s. Sandra Wallman is one researcher who is pioneering these kinds of studies in Inner London, and she claims 'there is no reason why the jobless could not build integrity and identity on the work of running a family and participating in community life, once these kinds of work were recognised to be socially and economically valuable. There is already massive evidence to show that some forms of "informal" economic activities fulfil these functions for some people'. (Henry 1981)

Our argument is that the arena for working out the balance for these different kinds of work is the locality and that it is unlikely that there will be much mobility between places in the coming decades. The place where one is born and brought up is likely to become a dominant source of consciousness for most people. It is there that they will encounter the local labour market, housing market and formal urban system, with varying consequences. There is a need to understand how the different forms of work outside employment articulate in a local milieu. All these elements help to produce a distinctive local consciousness with political consequences, which have yet to be fully charted. As we have seen, people use the trades unions and the professional associations for improving their position in the formal economy. But, by definition, these organisations are powerless in the informal area with which we have been concerned in this chapter. The question of power and control in the informal sector still has to be faced. The danger of mafia-style developments, with big bosses and thuggery, is clearly alarming. In Italy it has been claimed that between 10 and 35 percent of the labour force is involved in the informal economy, accounting for some 15 percent of the Gross Domestic Product. (In Britain, various estimates range between 2 and 7.5 percent of GDP.) The informal economy in this case is simply the economic activity not recorded in official statistics – what we broadly see as shadow wage labour or shadow petty commodity production. This area may indeed be growing faster than the so-called formal economy and it is likely to have its own shadow forms of regulation and control.

This chapter is more speculative than the previous three and that is inevitably so. Evidence from national time budget surveys or income and expenditure surveys can give some clues to the general problem, but unlike the local labour markets of the formal economy, upon which data can relatively easily be gathered, there is no parallel source of data which documents the undocumented work outside employment. However, there are many indications that as the formal economy contracts, this work will become more salient. Sceptics may argue that, as men do more domestic work, so such activity will become socially re-evaluated. We are arguing that the processes determining the *unstructured* aspects of urban life may be becoming more salient as the formal economy contracts and British society learns to live with much higher levels of unemployment than have been maintained for any length of time throughout the century.

Our suggestion is that the local configuration of work opportunities – defining work in its very broadest sense, as suggested in this chapter – will become more central to people's life-chances and will vary substantially from one part of the country to another. This may involve a rather different approach in urban sociology and urban geography. It will certainly have substantial implications for the practice of town planning and the activities of others in the social wage salariat. Whether the development of micro-processors will really mean that 'going to work' for many will involve little more than moving from the breakfast table to sit a few yards away in front of the television screen cannot be predicted with any certainty. There is no technical reason why one should not study for a degree, do a self-diagnosis medical check-up and order the weekly shopping by not moving from one's chair in front of the TV set. Whether such possibilities will reduce or increase the differences between places is hard to say. If formal employment takes up fewer and fewer hours of most people's time, then presumably other activities will come in to fill the void. A critical question for urban sociologists in the next twenty years will be to discover what urban life becomes when the structuring of formal employment may be substantially reduced.

8

APPROACHES TO URBAN POWER

Who gains, who loses?

So far in this book we have pointed to the forces which shape the
physical fabric and social structure of urban life. We have stressed the importance of economic change in the pattern of industrial–urban development, in the nature of employment, in the
housing market, and so on. We also noted that there are considerable spatial or territorial differences in the impact of these
forces. Patterns of spatial inequality and the social processes
through which certain resources are produced and allocated are a
major component of real income and life-chances which may
reinforce or mitigate inequalities generated directly in the labour
market. Thus each locality is a mosaic of opportunities and constraints resulting from the varying responses to these external
forces.

In this chapter we look more closely at people's attempts to
control or influence urban processes. How do local populations
cope with their circumstances? How can they intervene and
affect their immediate situation in relation to jobs, housing and
the environment? Are there major structural constraints which
compel certain actions and pre-empt others? Who benefits and
who loses from the operation of these constraints? Are there
some social groups who consistently manage to manipulate key
resources successfully? Which localities (and groups) benefit
least from the structures and processes of urban life? How do
they respond to their situation? How much influence can they
wield?

The central question which concerns us is the relative weight
of the several factors which explain local populations' life-

chances and the character and fate of urban areas: macro-economic and technological change over long periods; the action (and inaction) of capitalist investors (multi-national industries, large and small businesses, landowners, etc.); the activities of in-dividuals and groups as consumers and citizens (tenants, house-owners, tax-payers); and attempts by national and local state agencies to intervene in local economies and environments.

Essentially we are seeking to find out which person or interest effectively determines what happens. This may be a misplaced question, since it implies firstly that such a direct relationship between individuals or groups and outcomes is possible, and secondly that power is only about decisions which we perceive as opposed to all those about which we know nothing. The answer to the question 'who is running this town?' could indeed be 'no one' and such an answer could be a positive development in our understanding of urban power. The elusiveness and the ambi-guity of the concept of power has been the source of consider-able scholarly activity over the last twenty years, the main con-clusion of which is that much of what has passed as being knowl-edge of urban power is in fact more likely to be a mistake or a mystification. We now attempt to show why this should be so.

Market and plan in a local arena

Essentially, we argue that at the core of 'urban politics' is the in-teraction between capital and the state (or between market and plan rationality) and its effects on local populations. In advanced capitalist economies, political legitimacy and authority is largely dependent on the ability of the market and the state to deliver goods and resources, maintain living standards, protect certain values and interests, and reconcile competing claims and de-mands. Strategic decisions about resource allocation in both pri-vate and public sectors, and about the priority given to some political interest rather than others, reflect struggles for power and lead to further conflict. Thus faced with the threat of poli-tical unrest caused by poverty, disease and urban squalor (a con-sequence of unrestrained market capitalism), governments since the nineteenth century have conceded the necessity for some in-tervention in the economy, including the provision of some form of 'social wage'. These exigencies persist today and are given greater salience now by organised political activity at the local and national levels – political parties, pressure groups, and disparate 'urban social movements' (such as squatters groups, neighbourhood action groups, etc.).

Theorists disagree about whether the welfare state is a countervailing force against capitalism or merely an ameliorist solution to secure working class compliance, but the crucial point is that there are *contradictory* demands on central and local governments, and their interventions often compound existing inequalities or produce further variation in local conditions and opportunities. Efforts to equalise opportunities throughout the country (e.g. regional employment/industrial policy) and between groups (e.g. provision of council housing, rate rebates, etc.) may entail measures unacceptable to capitalists because they are regarded as interfering with private property and/or undermining profitability because of tax burdens. So, too, local council policies intended to generate prosperity for some areas and groups (e.g. urban planning decisions favouring office development or road construction rather than public housing) will be the object of conflict between opposed groups and interests. The outcome of these kinds of political processes is an uneven patchwork: social and spatial inequality in resources and life-chances.

Models of power in society

Questions about urban politics inevitably lead to a consideration of the concept of power. This has been one of the central concepts in sociology and the social sciences more generally, and has been at the centre of considerable controversy. Different models of the sources, distribution and use of power are inevitably closely tied up with particular views of society since power relations are the root of the mechanisms of stability and change. The issues that have been raised are complex, and beyond the scope of this chapter, but two points stand out.

The first is that there is considerable debate about the link between economic relations and power relations. Whilst in general few would dispute that economic relations are fundamental in determining outcomes, in particular cases different processes operate to produce different results. Thus different styles of management and political ideologies mediate between economic processes and outcomes. This is why different societies whose economic organisation is commonly capitalist produce as widely different political and social systems as Sweden and South Africa. It also needs to be recognised that the relations between economy and politics could take many forms – economic relations could be reflected in the sense that those who are economically dominant can consistently achieve their objectives, or they could be manifest in the ways by which opposing interests cannot achieve their goals because of economic constraints.

This leads on to the second point: that there are many ways in which power can be exercised. This has been a major theme of American political science debates, which extended the definitions of the sorts of actions which could be considered as forms of exercise of power. It is important to recognise that local urban power is manifested in many more forms than voting and debates in council. The most limited model, which is often labelled 'pluralist', and three extensions will be briefly noted below.

1. The decision-making model. The most limited model is concerned with overt conflicts over defined issues. It studies the process of decision-making in specific issues in order to determine who has power in a community, or indeed whether anyone has power. It is assumed that all groups who have interests in the issues are involved in the process, and thus that winners and losers can readily be identified. This model does not necessarily assume that everyone has equal power, but it does assume that everyone can have some influence over the outcome in issues that concern them.

2. The exclusion of interests model. A second model extends the concept of the exercise of power to cases where some views are systematically excluded from the decision-making process by the way issues are defined or by restrictions on access to the political system. Certain views may be defined as irrelevant, or the way they are expressed may be defined as irresponsible. Issues which are raised may be defined as beyond the scope of the decision-making institution. In these ways some groups who attempt to pursue their interests may be systematically thwarted, and other groups who are able to manipulate the situation in this way will be more likely to realise their interests.

3. The anticipated reactions model. The third model extends the concept of power yet further by including situations where issues are never raised, because of anticipated reactions. If it is assumed that a group or an institution will not respond to an issue being raised, or may even take coercive action against those raising it, then a grievance may never reach the political system. In the same way a group or corporation may have power in a local community without ever having to communicate with the local political institutions, if it is anticipated that the raising of an issue will cause its intervention. Crenson (1971), in a study of air pollution control in the United States, shows that just such a situation existed in the city of Gary, in the state of Indiana. Gary's industry was dominated by one steel firm, US Steel, whose reputation for power was such that the air pollution issue was not raised until 1962; while in the adjacent steel town of East Chicago, without a single large company, pollution control was introduced in 1949.

4. The mystification model. The first three models assume that people realise that they have an interest in an issue, whether or not they articulate it. However, there is a fourth extension of the concept of power, which concerns cases where people's real interests are affected without their realising it, or where problems are not perceived to be susceptible to political intervention. If there is a conflict over resources, those who do not realise the conflict is going on are likely to be the main losers.

All these approaches to power concern conflicts or non-conflicts within a political system in which one can define who the actors involved are. While the first two models superficially account for, say, local councils' planning decisions or housing policy, the other models provide more adequate explanations for the emergence or pre-emption of those decisions and their consequences for different groups' interests. However, in many cases 'local' politics can be understood as the 'working out' of wider processes. Thus the study of the operation of power cannot be restricted to the interaction of groups in a specific locality. Indeed, a major argument of this book has been that a locality will be subject to *processes* which have a major effect on life-chances, but which are outside local control. Thus it is impossible to focus on the local political system by studying local government as the sole place where decisions about the locality are made, as many political science studies of decision-making have assumed. The study of *urban* politics is not the same as the study of *local* politics.

Basically we are arguing that the analysis of urban power is not a question of understanding a structure of given power relationships, but rather recognising the process or, one might say, distinctive forces, which in general can be individually isolated and analysed, but which when brought together with the other forces or processes in a particular locality produce a distinctive result. Thus, what, as it were, 'happens' can be understood in terms of these general processes, even though there may be considerable variation in what happens from place to place. Different outcomes can be explained in terms of the same processes.

From the analysis of power to the study of the political system

Whilst these arguments would apply at any level of political analysis, we are concerned specifically with the problem of local urban autonomy and the state. The growth of the local state has been a major process of the last thirty years and it has become involved in more and more areas of urban life, and by becoming involved makes them the object of political conflict. However, two major points need to be recognised: first, the most important political processes affecting urban areas take place at the national level, and at the local level they may be experienced simply as constraints on what local populations can do; second, all political processes at both local and national level will be subject to economic processes, which place limits on what can be done.

Thus two central questions in urban politics are: how autonomous are localities and, which is the essence of politics, can politics control the economic or do economic questions control politics? The question of autonomy has clearly varied over time. We have already seen in the context of medieval York the moving of power to the centre, but during the period of rapid urban growth in the nineteenth century power appeared to flow to the large centres of industry and commerce such as Manchester and Birmingham. Now, with economic stagnation or decline, central government appears unwilling to allow local authorities even a modest amount of independence. Furthermore, it is possible, with a shift in the composition of government, that control to ensure that local authorities spend in what may be seen to be progressive ways will also be directed from the centre. This ebbing and flowing of power to and from the centre does seem to be related to economic change, but not in a mechanistic fashion. Hence the relative weight of economic forces and political forces remains a central topic of investigation. It is to the elaboration of these points that we now turn.

At a number of points in this book we have discussed urban processes which have their origin in central government political decision or the action of national political organisations. These will be briefly reiterated here. They have to be seen both as national urban political decisions and as decisions which will affect all local areas and be seen as constraints at that level.

1. *Expansion of state agencies and its consequences.* The most important underlying process has been the rapid growth of the state since 1945, and particularly the growth of the welfare state. This growth has been very largely driven by central government initiative, and it has forced a wider range of responsibilities on local bodies. It has a number of other possible consequences, including the politicisation of many areas of local state policy and a consequent growth in the number of protest movements, and the increasing unionisation and militancy of local state workers who are becoming an independent interest group.

2. *Reorganisation of political units.* There is a system of administrative structures and of boundaries, which have been determined from the centre. These are very important in determining what can be done within the locality. For example, as was shown in Chapter 6, there is a wide range of organisations operating in a given area. Many of these organisations are not locally elected, and the locally elected bodies have no ability to act over certain issues. (For example, since 1929 local bodies have had no responsibility for unemployment relief, and the bodies regulating

the labour market are generally not subject to local control.) Moreover, the legal structure of local government is such as to constrain what can be done. In general, a specific legal sanction has to exist before money can be spent on a service. There is also a two-tier system of elective local government which further limits the actions of the lower tier and opens up the possibility of political conflict between the tiers. Moreover, the system of boundaries can have consequences. There is a considerable body of literature on the operation of the zoning regulations in the United States which shows how, with a multiplicity of small authorities, some areas can act to keep low-income populations out by enforcing minimum housing densities. Something similar operates in Britain since, generally speaking, large cities with housing problems have rather narrowly defined boundaries, which means that the building of new housing often has to be in adjoining suburbs or rural authorities. Young and Kramer (1978) show how one suburban London borough was able to thwart plans by the GLC to build local authority housing to relieve inner London housing problems. Thus areas may not have resources, in this case building land, to pursue policies because of the way boundaries are drawn.

More generally, the operation of the town planning system, in combination with the structure of boundaries, has had a number of systematic effects on local areas. This is, in fact, a case where a central political decision has unintended consequences, because it was unable to alter fundamentally the way the market operated. Peter Hall and his colleagues (1973) have shown in their major study of the operations of the planning system, *The Containment of Urban England*, that the system is succeeding in preventing urban sprawl, but has had social consequences which were not foreseen by the policy makers. Its net effects have been extremely inegalitarian, with the main beneficiaries being the wealthiest owner-occupiers, those who live in rural areas, and anyone with a commercial interest in land and property. The losers have included most council tenants, the less well-off owner-occupiers and inner city private tenants.

As a result, many of the hopes that were entertained in the late 1960s about the way planning could be used as an egalitarian tool were illusory.

Donnison contrasts the optimism of the 1960s with the pessimism of the 1980s. It was assumed that:

> many of the nation's problems could in time be solved by redistributing a growing volume of resources between rich and poor people and poor cities and regions without any major group, interest or area suffering a real decline in living standards. A mild egalitarianism was therefore politically feasible, enabling mildly progressive politicians in all parties to gain the support of the electorate for programmes which promised to redistribute resources more equally... (Donnison 1981, p. 4).

The problem was that the real effect of the tools that were used for this purpose was to support the status quo. In the 1960s, the planning legislation operated systematically to protect and enhance property values.

3. Local reflections of national divisions. The groups and classes which are involved in local conflicts are also parts of national groups and classes. The cleavages in a local area will derive from national cleavages, and thus often from national definitions of issues. This is important because national definitions may not reflect local realities. For example, there is an ideologically very significant political cleavage between owner-occupiers and council tenants at the national level. If this is replicated at the local level, it may conceal a conflict of interests between council tenants and owner-occupiers in a high density area on the one hand, and low density owner-occupiers on the other.

4. Direct control by central institutions. There is a system of central control over local government which has a considerable influence over what is done. This operates particularly through the control over the resources available and the level of this control is increasing. Whereas in the past government placed limits on the proportion of local expenditure which could be met from central government grants, changes in 1980 sought to limit local expenditure by removing central grants from individual authorities which were deemed to have overspent. Currently there are proposals to take away the power of local councils even to set their own rates levels independently. Central government also exercises detailed supervision in a number of other areas, such as the specific approval of capital projects. There are also a number of other national influences on local government policy. For example, local political parties will follow the national party line on many local government issues. Moreover, the local authorities themselves have national associations which attempt to co-ordinate views. National organisations such as the trades unions and the Confederation of British Industry are also involved in local government issues.

5. *Expansion of nationally-based professions.* The growth of the local state has increased the number of bureaucratic and professional groups implementing local government policy. As we noted in Chapter 6, many of these professions in fact have a considerable influence over the policy that is pursued, and since these professions are nationally organised, exchange information and exert influence at this level, it is likely that some of these effects will operate systematically over all authorities.

National processes and local variations

These national factors are essential for an understanding of what happens in local areas, and if we look for urban power in the local area without considering them then the results will be somewhat misleading. As Dunleavy (1980) argues, it is difficult to explain changes which have affected all authorities over a short period of time if we look only at local decision-making. He cites the cases of the shifts in house-building policy to high-rise buildings in the 1960s and rehabilitation in the 1970s, or the shift to comprehensive education. These need to be explained in terms of a number of the above processes and also a number of market processes. These non-local urban policy changes may·have far more impact on people's everyday lives than do policy changes which are unambiguously local.

In spite of these structural constraints and central influences, there are still local variations and possibilities of independent local action as a result of strategies pursued by local political organisations. This can lead to major variations in the social wage provided by different authorities. For example, there are considerable variations in the level of subsidy provided to public transport and hence to fares and standards of services. In general, local initiatives result in a heterogeneous mixture of public provision in different areas. Some councils with one political structure may, for example, invest heavily in selective schools and commercial development whilst minimising public spending on other activities. Other councils will positively discriminate in favour of their working class constituents by providing massive public housing schemes. Research since the late 1960s suggests that there are some limited variations in the level of expenditure of Labour and Conservative parties on different services, with Labour-controlled authorities in general spending more on housing and education, while Conservative authorities spend somewhat more than average on highways, welfare services and the police.

There is a further source of variation which may be even more important that these political variations. The expansion of the local state has given local authority bureaucrats and professions greater scope for discretion in the exercise of their functions and the allocation of resources. Though they cannot be seen as independent of economic processes and central government decisions, different management styles do make a considerable difference in the outcomes in different areas. One example is the dispute between county police forces such as Devon and Cornwall, which stress community policing as a means of preventing trouble occurring, and those such as Greater Manchester, which stress the importance of a highly equipped police force able to respond quickly and vigorously to trouble when it does occur. Variations in management style extend to all areas of local government policy and they are manifested in a number of different ways. For example, councils may be more or less responsive to pressure from local residents over details of policy implementation, such as housing and development schemes (for one example see Davies 1972). They may have strong independent departments with a preference for innovation and the growth of service provision or a more centralised structure which emphasises control over expenditure. The growth of the local state has been a process operating over the whole country, but the way it has been implemented has varied from area to area, and the differences of managerial style have persisted over relatively long periods. They are an important element in the variations in the life-chances of different populations.

In view of these sorts of variations it is important to understand how local urban politics operate in practice. Regrettably, there are relatively few recent detailed published studies of 'community power' in Britain (some are listed in the references), and hardly any which explicitly consider the relative importance of national/central versus local factors. Evidence from the National Community Development Projects or Lambert *et al.*'s (1978) study of housing in Birmingham indicates the importance of 'macro' factors for local politics. However, the complexities of urban power as the resultant of both central and local forces can be seen by looking at one study in detail.

Politics in Croydon as a resultant of forces

One of the major local studies of urban politics in recent years has been that by Peter Saunders of Croydon, a borough in the southern suburbs of London, carried out in the early 1970s (Saunders 1979).

Croydon has a mixed population, with a substantial lower income and working class area in the north, and a large area of low density middle-class housing in the south of the borough. Croydon also contained the largest concentration of commercial office space in southern England outside central London. Local government was dominated by the Conservative Party, who had a very secure majority. The Labour minority on the council had little expectation of ever gaining control. Saunders argues that power within the council was very highly centralised. Within the Conservative group he identifies a political elite, which held most of the committee chairmanships, and controlled the Policy Sub-Committee, which co-ordinated overall council policy. There were relatively few occasions on which 'backbench' Conservative councillors could prevail against this elite.

Saunders's main concern was with the relations between the council and the three major groups noted above – the middle class residents of the south, the working class residents of the north and the commercial business interests – and to see how far they influenced council policy. The groups will be considered in turn, though in practice their interests cannot be simply separated, since gains by one group were often losses by another.

The middle class of south Croydon

The southern middle class was very highly organised. Eight groups made up the Federation of South Croydon Residents Associations, with a total membership of 17,000. Each ward had at least one residents association, one of which claimed a membership of 95 percent of eligible families. On occasions this strength was mobilised, but the most usual forms of political activity were on a personal basis. The southern residents had a very wide range of personal contacts on which they could call. For example, most Conservative councillors, whether they represented northern or southern wards, lived in the south. These contacts constituted a considerable political resource, and could be used to pass opinions to the council and to gather information about council plans. There were two major interests which southern residents sought to protect. One was the maintenance of a low level of rates, since their demand for council services was generally very low and rateable values were very high. The second interest was the prevention of new housing development in the area, particularly development, either public or private, at densities above the very low levels prevailing in south Croydon. Such development might have constituted a threat to property values in the area.

Saunders shows that on the whole they were very successful in protecting these interests. Many private building schemes were rejected by the council as being at too high a density. Housing developments at fifty or seventy people per acre were being accepted in the north, while in the south schemes were passed at fifteen people per acre. A proposal to develop an area at a density of six houses per acre was rejected, and the developer eventually gained acceptance for a scheme at under four houses per acre. The justification for this approach was the need to protect open space in an area of natural beauty, and appeal was made to the principle of maintaining the Green Belt. Such views were fully endorsed by the Croydon council and the council's representatives relayed them to the Greater London Council as arguments against using Croydon's land to solve London's housing problems.

There were occasions on which the southern residents mobilised in an overt manner, with campaigns in the press and protest meetings. One example was over a development proposal by a large private education trust, the Whitgift Foundation, with extensive commercial interests in central Croydon and close ties with the council. The proposal, in addition to building houses, would have expanded the number of private education places in the borough. The success of this resistance, which defeated an organisation with a considerable reputation for power in Croydon and went against the major interest of Croydon Conservatives in private education, shows the power of the southern residents. There were other instances where the southern residents mobilised against the council. Cases include planning applications which had gone to central government to be determined and the shift to comprehensive education. Saunders argues that these are cases of tactical protest whose aim was not so much to attack council policy as to strengthen the hand of groups on the council who were trying to resist implementation of policies imposed by other government organisations.

The working class of north Croydon

The southern middle class in Croydon engaged in a consistent and generally very successful urban movement to protect their interests, but who were the losers? It would appear that their victories were not at the expense of the local government organisation but, in many cases, at the expense of the residents of the north of the borough. The low densities imposed on housing developments in south Croydon meant that very little new council housing or lower priced private housing was built for those trying to move out of the higher density areas of the north. The successful maintenance of a low rate policy reduced the services available to those who did need them. Saunders shows that in most areas of social policy Croydon adopted a policy of low spending and that its services were criticised in central government reports as being of low quality. The borough consistently ranked among the lowest London boroughs in terms of council housing completions, while ranking amongst the highest for private housing completions. In the early 1970s Croydon's social services expenditure was less than 70 percent of the per capita average in London, leading to below average standards of provision of such services as day nurseries, meals-on-wheels and home helps for the disabled.

What means did working class residents have to influence the council to improve this situation? Saunders considers two categories of means. The first involved working through organisations which used accepted channels of access to the council, while the second involved resorting to direct action.

Of the first, the Labour Party was much the most important, but it was very limited in the extent to which it could effectively change the situation. In the first place, the Labour Party was always a minority on the council. It was thus limited in the number of concessions it could extract from the Conservative majority. Moreover, the Labour councillors were becoming increasingly middle class in the early 1970s and less directly in touch with working-class interests. There was often a conflict between the socialism of the middle class councillors and what they saw as the traditional parochialism of their constituents. This was shown in the issue of council house sales, where many council tenants were broadly in favour and the Labour Party strongly opposed.

The tenants' associations were another channel by which local authority tenants sought to influence the council and in some issues, such as the provision of a community centre or the banning of heavy lorries from residential streets, they could be relatively successful. However, they tended to retreat from more contentious issues; one, for example, took no position on two of the major issues affecting its members: the question of where a new school should be built and the sale of council houses on the estate. Saunders argues that the tenants' associations dealt with the council strictly on its terms, and they had little to say over a wide range of issues. In addition to the Labour Party and the tenants' associations, there were a number of *ad hoc* pressure groups in Croydon. Such groups had a problem in not having established channels of communication with the council. This meant that they had difficulties both in finding out what the council planned to do and also in persuading it to listen to them. Saunders did, however, find examples of successful pressure groups, notably one campaigning for a day nursery in north

Croydon. The success of this group depended on three factors. The first was the ability to incur costs in time, money and energy in mounting the campaign. The second was the ability to steer a course between putting pressure on the councils and staying within the 'rules of the game' and not appearing as a challenge to the legitimacy of the council's authority. Thirdly, the demand was in fact very limited, and what was gained was not a major change in the council's policy of low expenditure on social services. The case of the Labour Party, the tenants' associations and the 'responsible' protest movements suggests that the gains which were made through 'legitimate' channels of influence were very limited. The same would also appear to be the case of more direct forms of protest. There were cases of demonstrations at council meetings and squatting movements to protest at housing policy, but these lacked solid backing and were too easily branded as irresponsible. Saunders concludes that in Croydon the working class found it impossible to create a movement to win gains from the council, which was not either incorporated into the council and thus limited in what it would demand, or else one which was forced to articulate its demands in such a way that they were rejected as illegitimate.

Property development in Croydon

The group which has made the greatest gains from Croydon council policy in the post-war years has been the commercial business sector. The starting point was the purchase of a relatively small site for a road scheme, which was achieved through a Private Act of Parliament in 1956, which also enabled the council to develop or sell the land not required for the road. The success of the first such scheme created enormous demand, and, in the next few years, the council searched for further sites to develop. By the mid-1960s central Croydon contained more than fifty large office blocks and a total office space of 5 million square feet. The firms were taking advantage of low rents by comparison with central London, low rates, relatively low wage rates and Croydon's very good communications. The council's role in this was in finding sites and the provision of related infrastructure, particularly roads and car parks. This meant that in the early 1970s, at the same time as the council was cutting back on social service expenditure, it was incurring new expenditure for car parking plans.

The council identified the interests of business with the interests of Croydon. The extra rate revenue may have helped justify this, but the development did not benefit all Croydon's residents. Directly affected were the people whose houses were acquired in order to build roads. Indirectly, the cost of these programmes, when combined with a low rate policy, was at the expense of those demanding council services. Another group of losers were local industrialists and shopkeepers. The former were concerned at the effect on the supply of labour for manufacturing industry, and also at the shortage of industrial land in the borough, whilst the latter were seriously affected by competition from the new shopping centre associated with the office building.

Thus, paradoxically, the actions of the local council benefited outside commercial interests at the expense of local businessmen. This is particularly surprising given that the latter group was well represented on the council. It is clear that development was not simply accidental. The council's initial role was active, and council leaders reiterated their commitment to development. Saunders argues that one important factor was the crucial role of one leading member of the council, Sir James Marshall, who urged the use of the Private Act in 1956. He was also the chairman of the Whitgift Foundation, and in this role was responsible for one of the largest redevelopments, the Whitgift Centre, involving 537,000 square feet of office space and 460,000 square feet of shops. Oliver Marriott, in his book on the property boom in Britain, assesses his role thus:

This practical approach to the replanning of Croydon reflects the driving force of one man, Sir James Marshall . . . Although an elected representative rather than an official, this hard-headed autocrat was in a sense comparable to an American-style town boss. What Marshall said, went. Extremely commercially minded, and an orthodox Conservative, he was, as it were, the managing director of Croydon. (Marriott 1967, 185–6).

Thus the development of Croydon cannot be accounted for as the result of conflicts between interests, for it was largely based on the council *anticipating* the requirements of business. In later years, however, Saunders found that although large business was not particularly strongly represented on the council, there were considerable contacts between leading councillors and senior executives of the firms. These contacts were often as members of the same voluntary and charitable organisations, such as the Rotary Club, or more formal bodies, such as the board of governors of the technical college. There was a small core of organisational leaders embracing council and business which was 'self-selecting, self-perpetuating and exclusive'. The kinds of benefits derived from this sort of contact may appear to be relatively modest, such as the resiting of bus stops or direct access from a multi-storey car park into a store. However, Saunders stresses the importance of shared political values and argues that the main aim is to ensure predictability for the businesses and the creation of a favourable political climate in the long term.

A number of important points about urban politics arises from the Croydon study. The first is simply that there were major distributive consequences of the council's policies. Local decisions made a considerable difference to the life-chances of sections of the population and, to a very large extent, the decisions that were made served to increase inequalities. Second, and related to this, different sections of the population had different degrees of access to the council and influence over its policies, and some groups had very little to say in what went on at all. Third, the actions of one local movement were usually at the expense of the other sections of the population. Fourth, those who benefited were not necessarily local people or firms, but often commercial businesses moving into Croydon. However, Croydon is only one case study and it is probable that in other areas a different balance of political forces would lead to different groups gaining and losing. It is also important to note that Croydon was an economically buoyant area and the council, although it made decisions independently, was taking advantage of underlying economic conditions. It is probable that the freedom of action of a local council would be much less in a depressed area or in an economic recession. Croydon could have redistributed wealth in a more egalitarian fashion, for example by levying higher rates and providing more services, though it did not. Other areas do not have the wealth to redistribute.

The elephant's foot?

Studies such as that of Croydon may, by analogy, be likened to studying an elephant's foot to try to understand the elephant as a whole. The foot, the outcome of processes and structure in the local area, is all that can be seen of the elephant on the ground. Local studies are misleading if it is not realised that what is seen is part of something larger, but the analysis of the foot can tell us something about the elephant as a whole, though by no means everything.

The difficulty of coming to terms with the slippery concept of power which is experienced by urban sociologists is experienced in a different way by people in our towns and cities who resent either the imposition or the lack of some aspect of the urban infrastructure, but find difficulty in grasping, or indeed finding, the levers which could change it. Feelings of frustration can lead some people to migrate to areas with better facilities or fewer impositions. Those without that option may become so frustrated that violent action is all that is left to them. The middle way of voting in an alternative council is rarely regarded as an effective option. The low voting figures in local government elections is a political fact of much significance and is a statement about the distribution of power.

The theoretical analysis of urban power coupled with the response of people in cities demonstrates a serious contradiction. The credibility gap between the notion that people should be able to have more control over the local worlds in which they live and the practice by which such control has been more and more taken away will produce a frustration or alienation in which something will have to give. Our sociological analysis points to an instability which will be reflected sporadically in acute urban conflict over the next decade.

9

CONCLUSIONS

People on their backs or people fighting back?

The urban arena is not only the resultant of wider processes, it
in turn generates its own social force. Imagine a meeting in an
inner city area which has just been the scene of violence and
looting. The people in the room will see quite different images of
the urban. The representative of one of the looted chain stores
will be considering the level of his losses, the problem of increasing insurance premiums and the possibility of shifting his investment elsewhere. The planner will think of the physical fabric
and have in mind her plan for refurbishing and redevelopment.
She will be aware of the crumbling façades, the decaying infrastructure of sewers and roads, and the need for more investment.
The social worker will think of the area as the source of a heavy
load of cases. He will think of individuals and families struggling
to cope with too little money and little likelihood that things will
get better. An industrialist, encouraged to attend the meeting by
some powerful person outside the area, sees it as an area of
low skills, possible labour militancy and a difficult site to develop, involving an awkward journey to work for his managers.
It would not be difficult to imagine the thoughts of the other
people who might be at such a meeting – the local general prac-
titioners, representatives from local historical and amenity
societies, or those anxious to excavate 'the medieval core of the
city', the local councillors and local MPs, concerned about being
re-elected, the chief of police for the area, community workers
and clergyman, housing managers and representatives from the
Trades Council and the Rotary Club, youth workers and leaders

of other youth organisations, teachers and representatives of the Education Department, local dignitaries – magistrates, landowners or those with 'family connections' in the area or those associated with housing associations – local political activists, students, researchers, and even some who have read this book. The list could easily and plausibly be extended for another page and in no case would it be difficult to imagine what is likely to be in the minds of those there. Let us assume we have got all these different views, fears, ideas, fallacies, misconceptions and insights in our head. We may then remember that not one of the people need necessarily live in the area in question. The clergyman is most likely to do so and the business leaders and dignitaries least likely to. If we have successfully understood not only what is in the minds of all these people, but also the degree of power and influence they have severally and collectively to affect what goes on in this city, we will, of course, know a great deal. This book may help to structure an understanding of the forces and processes that such people represent. We can understand how the household, which is a cause for concern to the social worker, is seen by the employer as simply unskilled labour, probably unemployable.

However, if all we see is so many roles, positions, institutions, structures and processes, we may end up with much knowledge and little understanding. We can provide systematic accounts derived from knowledge of housing tenure, local authority committee minutes, returns made to the Department of Employment or whatever: such exercises in abstraction, which have been the themes of previous chapters, have inevitably taken us a long way from the kerb level. If we return to our meeting, there is surely something a little odd about our account which focussed on all the officials and representatives of this and that but had nothing at all to say about what was in the heads of the people who were at the meeting – simply because they lived in the area and for no other reason. It would be a curious sociology which described the ideologies of the management, ignored the workers and then claimed that this was an adequate basis for a knowledge of the structures and processes of industrial life. Clearly, the actual experience of industrial or urban life by those who are most disadvantaged cannot be distilled from an accumulation of professionals' partial perspectives. A description of housing markets, labour markets and different kinds of work sets the scene but does not bring the play to life.

People's experience of the place they live in comes from what they actually experience in the events of their ordinary everyday life. The familiar faces of their local social networks help to structure their experience. They see programmes on TV in the context of their families and the friends they meet in pubs or outside the school gates. Their experience of wage labour is in the context of the others they share the experience with. Their expectation of work is mediated to them by what they first hear from their families and friends. People are conscious of the history of the place they live in, even when most landmarks to their past are destroyed. Famous football teams, a works that once dominated an area, the 'local' pub, familiar streets, bus routes and cafes all give style and a particular feel to a place. Moving to another city or another part of the same city breaks the continuity until a new set of social landmarks emerges.

We have emphasised the constraints of housing and labour markets, the domination of a 'formal' urban system and the gatekeepers who control access to a whole range of urban resources and facilities. This approach makes 'the urban' appear as a set of forces which weigh upon the people. The local state, the police, the welfare state, the enabling (or, as some would have it, *disabling*) professions handle their clients, cases, patients, applicants, claimants, kids, youths, old people and problems of all descriptions. But of course we know that when we talk of 'the managing of everyday life' we are referring primarily to the management of people who have little else but the capacity to sell their labour power for a wage. Chapters 4, 5 and 6 were about the structures and processes of urban life that dominate ordinary working people.

We thus come to a curious paradox. Throughout much of urban life the city dweller or citizen was distinct from ordinary working people. The Burgher or Bourgeois was a superior person. The city dweller was sophisticated and cosmopolitan. But now we are saying that urban life is a controlled and organised life for the mass of ordinary working people and it is they who are the typical urban dwellers. The contemporary bourgeoisie are more likely to live in suburbs or outside the towns and those living in the centre at least have a 'weekend cottage' to which they can retreat. So, in Britain, the basis of working class culture has become urban. Unlike countries which have urbanised later, like France or even the United States, the English working class does not have a peasant or small town background to provide a sort of cultural datum. This is not to say that rural-type activities such as keeping pigeons or ferrets are not common, but they are definitely rural-type pursuits of urban people.

Urban sociologists are returning to the study of detailed ethnography of local populations after a decade or more of neglect. Stimulated by the ideas of the Birmingham Centre for Contemporary Cultural Studies, a new generation of researchers is less prepared to accept overly structural determination of people's activities. They are reacting to a kind of sociology which was fashionable in the mid 1970s, which left people as puppets bobbing up and down to the strings of monopoly capitalism and the 'oppressive state apparatus'. We do not dispute that the way our society works *is* constraining and dominating for most ordinary people. The work they do demands little skill and responsibility and is frequently noisy, dirty and even dangerous. Huge lorries thunder through city streets and the visual environment of the 'parades' of shops in the suburbs or the heap of supermarkets in the centre is often squalid and degrading. Council estates give a drab and dreary impression, in marked contrast to the diversity and interest often found in middle class suburbs. But, having said that, we return to our opening sentence. People are not crushed into passive submission. They create their own worlds despite the enveloping structures and processes we have described. People make their own history and their own urban life: it is not *all* made for them.

The curious thing is that although sociologists recognise the distinctiveness and importance of working-class culture, they have been slower to come to a deeper understanding of it than of the other matters we have discussed in this book. One thing is, however, very clear: there is no single working-class culture which unites ordinary working people wherever they are. Rather, there are distinctive working-class cultures which are *local* and tied to places and regions. The nature and range of jobs that have been and are available is of crucial importance. Working-class consciousness on Tyneside is tied to the experience of a declining engineering and shipbuilding industry. The names of the big industrialists, once dominant and powerful fifty years ago, are known and remembered, and such knowledge colours the way people respond to current circumstances. Similarly, workers in south Essex have been moulded by their experience of working for Fords over the generations. Different work experiences, different forms of conflict or incorporation and different employment opportunities produce distinctive responses. In areas which have not been dominated by a single employer or industry, other social elements provide continuity. With a long and varied history of stable and diverse employment, a working-class population can get well-rooted in an area. Generations go to school together and are not obliged to leave the area to find employment. So they marry locally and attend each other's weddings. Family events become community events: the local paper telling of births, deaths and marriages provides the most salient news. The faces in the pubs, the church hall jumble sales and the cafes are familiar. Local social networks are tightly enmeshed and, since women typically control the power based on kin, they may feel, and indeed be, less powerless than in newly settled areas.

We are now referring to working-class practices and our argument may be summarised in Fig 9.1. The distinctive cultural practices of working-class life do not wobble about according to the fads and fashions of the mass media, as some would argue. This is because the experience is mediated through a local context and, by definition, the mass media cannot cover the whole

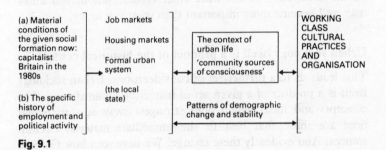

Fig. 9.1

range of distinctive experiences and contexts at the same time. Hence, there is generally a disjunction between the general and the specific or the national and the local. Overwhelmingly, working-class life is family life and such a life has to be lived in specific contexts. If the knowledge about markets and bureaucracies, which this book is about, is to develop into understanding, then it must be put into a local context of distinctive working-class cultural practices. This must involve a substantial amount of historical knowledge and understanding and, now, increasing knowledge and understanding of ethnic differences and practices. Other local symbols than pub or chapel have to be incorporated into such an understanding. In the same way that it is misleading to view the working class through the eyes of male chief earners, so it is equally misleading to view it entirely through the eyes of white anglo-saxons.

Our towns and cities will change over the next few decades and we can be certain about that because our knowledge of urban history confirms that urban change and conflict is the normal expectation. This change will not be a mechanistic one-way flow from the structures of markets to the families who are submissively acted upon. Rather, we must recognise that people play a part in creating their own history. Working-class consciousness and political action emerge from distinctive contexts.

It is arguable that the local context will have greater salience in the 1980s than it had in the middle of the century when employment was such a distinctive determinant of life-chances. As formal employment declines, and as deskilling of male manual workers continues, it is increasingly implausible to see the link between the household and the economy as being based entirely on the occupation of the male chief earner. Whom you know may well become more important than what you know.

Urban sociology itself is a product of the historical context

This leads us to a further set of considerations. Urban sociology itself is a product of a given set of historical circumstances. The concepts and ideas which hold strongest sway at a particular time are those that best fit the immediate material circumstances. And evidently these change. We have seen how Chicago in the 1920s was the scene for the development of a distinctive ecological approach. This was associated with a rapidly expanding capitalism, which provided the motor for change in the Central Business District, which expanded into the Zone of Transition. Similarly, the waves of new and diverse migrants into the city did much to produce its mosaic of social worlds.

In Britain in the 1960s, by contrast, the welfare state was rapidly expanding in all directions. Perhaps not surprisingly, this was the era of 'urban managerialism' which carried on to the mid-1970s. The focus was then on the constraining power of bureaucracies and their agents. The 'gatekeepers' still figure prominently in this book. However, towards the middle of the 1970s it became clear that 'the urban fiscal crisis' was not to be explained by the style of the managers. By analogy, that would imply that when a firm closed down as a result of a change in world market conditions it would be appropriate to blame the personnel manager. Evidently the asset-stripping boom of the early 1970s was following a logic which produced greater profit from land and property than from labour and manufacturing. The growth of multi-national companies and the takeover of much of British industry by external capital led to an awareness of the broader structural forces which could not be controlled locally. Perhaps the most symbolic and significant example of this process was the dramatic increase in oil prices after 1973. So urban sociology in the 1970s inevitably became more concerned with the climate and less concerned with the pool, to revert to our previous analogy (p. 60). Probably the most influential book of this period was *The Urban Question* by Manuel Castells, although many people found it easier to approach his ideas through his commentators and critics, such as C. G. Pickvance and Peter Saunders. Those who are stimulated by this book to deepen their understanding of the field will find Peter Saunders's book, *Social Theory and the Urban Question* (1981), a most valuable guide to debates which are not appropriately considered here.

However, the urban sociology of the 1980s will be different again from that of the 1960s and the 1970s. The shift from managerialism to structuralism did not fit the decades as closely as that and the pivotal years were more likely 1967, when *Race,*

Community and Conflict was published, and the mid-1970s, when the so-called 'new' urban sociology had its heyday. The *International Journal of Urban and Regional Research*, which serves as a focus for much of the more radical new work, began in 1977 and reflects the substantial shift of thinking over the previous decade. In 1981 this *Journal* published a powerful article by Professor Ivan Szelenyi of the University of Wisconsin, who is one of the most creative urban sociologists of his generation in the world. He argued that the wave of the new urban sociology of the 1970s based on structuralism was now over. It had served its purpose in the material circumstances of the time, but now there was a need to face a new agenda with different questions. He, too, reacted against the over-determinism of previous years and directed thinking towards new areas, such as the domestic/ informal economy or the distinctiveness of urban life under socialism.

We argue, therefore, that it is important to put ideas in context. What counts as 'urban' for urban sociologists will change over time as the arguments and intellectual focus also change. As Chapter 7 shows, we suggest that a greater concern with how ordinary people 'get by' will come to have more salience as structural unemployment makes its impact through the 1980s. The insights generated during earlier debates will still inform those debates which are yet to come, but as the material circumstances change, so too will concepts and ideas. We see this book less as a review of a body of knowledge which is firmly established, but rather more an introduction to a way of looking at the structures and processes of urban life.

Britain was the first nation to cope with the problem of urban – industrial society. Yet even by the last decades of the nineteenth century Britain was starting to lose her industrial pre-eminence. Economists now talk about de-industrialisation as a process which can be described and understood. We have not yet started to talk about de-urbanisation in the same way. However, as the material forces which produced huge new industrial complexes and the urban infrastructure to support them change, so too must the contexts. As we have hinted in Chapter 7 and, again, in this Conclusion, we may be facing new processes involving the renegotiation of the social division of labour. How the work is done and who does it may have to change. The impact of this on urban life may well be the theme for the coming wave of urban social theory. So theory and practice will interrelate in a never-ending dialectic. The structures and processes of urban life in the 1980s and 1990s will change but their style of interaction will remain the same. Such is the paradox of all sociology.

The way to done and who does it may have to change. The important thing an urban life may well be the theme for the coming

relate that and arguing the reactions and the sometime of urban life in the 1980s and 1990s will change and changed of urbanization will remain the same. Such pattern refresh of an sociology.

REFERENCES AND FURTHER READING

General

The following titles are important for developing a better understanding of the main themes of this book.

Castells, M. (1977) *The Urban Question*, Edward Arnold
Castells, M. (1978) *City, Class and Power*, Macmillan
Dear, M. and Scott, A. J. (eds) (1981) *Urbanisation and Urban Planning in Capitalist Society*, Methuen
Dunleavy, P. (1980) *Urban Political Analysis*, Macmillan
Harloe, M. (ed) (1977) *Captive Cities*, John Wiley
Harloe, M. and Lebas, E. (eds) (1981) *City, Class and Capital*, Edward Arnold
Harvey, D. (1973) *Social Justice and the City*, Edward Arnold
Lambert, C. and Weir, D. (eds) (1975) *Cities in Modern Britain*, Fontana
Mellor, R. (1977) *Urban Sociology in an Urbanised Society*, Routledge and Kegan Paul
Pahl, R. E. (1975) *Whose City?* (2nd edn), Penguin
Pickvance, C. G. (ed) (1976) *Urban Sociology: Critical Essays*, Tavistock
Saunders, P. (1979) *Urban Politics: a Sociological Interpretation*, Hutchinson
Saunders, P. (1981) *Social Theory and the Urban Question*, Hutchinson

Open University Course D202, *Urban Change and Conflict*

Chapter 1 The origins and growth of pre-industrial urbanism in Britain

Abrams, P. and Wrigley, E. A. (eds) (1978) *Towns in Societies*, Cambridge University Press
Benton, J. F. (ed) (1968) *Town Origins: the evidence from Medieval England*, D. C. Heath; Harrap
Clark, P. and Slack, P. (1976) *English Towns in Transition 1500–1700*, Oxford University Press
Fisher, F. J. (1948) The development of London as a centre of conspicuous consumption in the sixteenth and seventeenth centuries, *Trans. Royal Historical Society*, 4th ser., **30**, 37–50

Lowenstein, S. F. (1965) 'Urban images of Roman authors', *Comparative Studies in Society and History*, **8**, 110–23

Miller, Edward (1961) 'Medieval York' in Tillott P. M. (ed), *A History of Yorkshire: The City of York*, Oxford University Press

Phythian-Adams, C. (1972) 'Ceremony and the citizen: the communal year at Coventry 1450–1550' in Clark, P. and Slack, P. (eds) *Crisis and Order in English Towns 1500–1700*, 57–85, London

Phythian-Adams, C. (1978) 'Urban decay in late Medieval England' in P. Abrams and E. A. Wrigley (eds) *op. cit.*, 159–86

Pirenne, H. (1925) *Medieval Cities* (new edn), Doubleday Anchor Books, 1956

Sjoberg, G. (1960) *The Preindustrial City*, The Free Press of Glencoe

Tacitus (trans. 1948) *On Britain and Germany* (trans. H. Mattingley), Penguin Books

Thrupp, Sylvia L. (1948) *The Merchant Class of Medieval London*, University of Michigan Press; Ann Arbor paperbacks, 1962

Weber, M. (1921: trans. 1958) *The City*, Heinemann, 1958 (first published in German, 1921)

Williams, R. (1973) *The Country and the City*, Chatto and Windus

Wrigley, E. A. (1978) 'A simple model of London's importance in changing English society and economy 1650–1750' in Abrams, P. and Wrigley, E. A. *op. cit.*, 215–44

Chapter 2 The emergence of industrial urbanism in Britain

Anderson, M. (1971) *Family Life in Nineteenth Century Lancashire*, Cambridge University Press

Ashworth, William (1954) *The Genesis of Modern British Town Planning*, Routledge

Briggs, Asa (1968) *Victorian Cities* (rev. edn), Penguin Books

Chalmers, T. (1820–?) *The Christian and Civic Economy of Large Towns*, 3 vols, London

Checkland, S. G. (1964) 'The British industrial city as history: the Glasgow case', *Urban Studies*, **1**, 34–54

Davies, C. S. (1963) *North Country Bred*, Routledge

Dyos H. J. (ed) (1968) *The Study of Urban History*, Edward Arnold

Engels, F. (1845) *The Condition of the Working Class in England*

Foster, J. (1968) 'Nineteenth century towns – a class dimension' in Dyos, *op. cit.*

Foster, J. (1974) *Class Struggle and the Industrial Revolution*, Methuen

Glass, R. (1968) 'Urban Sociology in Great Britain' in Pahl, R. E. (ed), *Readings in Sociology*, Pergamon Press

Hammond, J. L. and Hammond, B. (1917; 2nd edn, 1925) *The Town Labourer 1760–1832*, Longman; reprint edn, 1966

Laslett, Peter (1965) *The World We Have Lost*, Methuen

Marshall, J. D. (1968) 'Colonisation as a factor in the planting of towns in North-West England' in Dyos, *op. cit.*

Meacham, S. (1977) *A Life Apart: The English Working Class 1890–1914*, Thames and Hudson

Roberts, R. (1973) *The Classic Slum*, Penguin

Stedman Jones, G. (1971) *Outcast London*, Oxford University Press

Stedman Jones, G. (1974) 'Working class culture and working class politics in London 1870–1900', *Journal of Social History*, **8**, 460–508

Thompson, P. (1975) *The Edwardians*, Weidenfeld and Nicholson

Tilly, L. A. and Scott, J. W. (1978) *Women, Work and Family*, Holt, Rinehart and Winston

Weber, A. F. (1899) *The Growth of Cities in the Nineteenth Century*; reprint edn, Cornell Paperbacks (OUP)

White, J. (1980) *Rothschild Buildings: Life in an East End Tenement Block 1887–1920*, Routledge and Kegan Paul

Chapter 3 Patterns of urban life?

Boal, F. W. (1974) 'Territoriality in Belfast' in Bell, C. and Newby, H. (eds), *The Sociology of Community*, Frank Cass

Boal, F. W., Murray, R. C. and Poole, M. A. (1976) 'Belfast: the urban encapsulation of a national conflict' in Glass, S. C. and Obler, J. L. (eds), *Urban Ethnic Conflict: A Comparative Perspective*, University of North Carolina, Chapel Hill

Burgess, E. W. (1925) 'The growth of the city' in Park, R. E. *et al. The City*, University of Chicago Press (reprinted 1967)

Davies, J. G. and Taylor, J. (1970) 'Race, community and no conflict', *New Society*, **16**, 67–69

George, M. Dorothy (1965) *London Life in the Eighteenth Century*, Penguin. (First published Kegan Paul, Trench, Trubner, 1925)

Park, R. E. (1952) *Human Communities*, Free Press of Glencoe

Park, R. E., Burgess, E. W. and Mackenzie, R. D. (1925) *The City*, University of Chicago Press (reprinted 1967)

Rex, J. and Moore, R. (1967) *Race, Community and Conflict*, Oxford University Press

Rex, J. and Tomlinson, S. (1979) *Colonial Immigrants in a British City*, Routledge and Kegan Paul

Shepherd, J., Westaway, J. and Lee, T. (1974) *A Social Atlas of London*, Oxford University Press

Theodorson, G. A. (ed) (1961) *Studies in Human Ecology*, Row, Peterson

Ward, R. H. (1978) 'Race relations in Britain', *British Journal of Sociology*, **29**, 4

Zorbaugh, H. W. (1929) *The Gold Coast and the Slum*, Chicago University Press

Chapter 4 The housing market

Damer, S. (1974) 'Wine alley: the sociology of a dreadful enclosure', *Sociological Review* (22), **2**, 221–48

Damer, S. (1976) 'A note on housing allocation' in Edwards, M. *et al.* (eds) *Housing and Class in Britain* Conference of Socialist Economists, London

Dunleavy, P. (1979) 'The urban basis of political alignment', *British Journal of Political Science*, **9**, 409–43

Goffman, E. (1968) *Asylums*, Penguin, Harmondsworth

Haddon, R. (1970) 'A Minority in the Welfare State', *New Atlantis*, **2**, 80–133

Lambert, J., Paris, C. and Blackaby, B. (1978) *Housing Policy and the State*, Macmillan, London

Lansley, S. (1979) *Housing and Public Policy*, Croom Helm, London

Mellor, J. R. (1977) *Urban Sociology in an Urbanised Society*, Routledge and Kegan Paul, London

Murie, A., Niner, P. and Watson, C. (1976) *Housing Policy and the Housing System*, George Allen and Unwin

Pahl, R. E. (1975) *Whose City?* (2nd edn), Penguin, Harmondsworth

Rex, J. and Moore, R. (1967) *Race, Community and Conflict*, Oxford University Press, London

Rex, J. and Tomlinson, S. (1979) *Colonial Immigrants in a British City*, Routledge and Kegan Paul, London

Saunders, P. (1979) *Urban Politics: a sociological interpretation*, Hutchinson, London

Chapter 5 The local labour market

Barron, R. D. and Norris, G. M. (1976) 'Sexual divisions and the dual labour market' in Barker, D. L. and Allen, S. (eds), *Dependence and Exploitation in Work and Marriage*, Longman, London

Blackburn, R. M. and Mann, M. (1979) *The Working Class in the Labour Market*, Macmillan, London

CDP (1977a) *The Costs of Industrial Change*, Inter Project Editorial Team, London

CDP (1977b) *Gilding the Ghetto*, Inter Project Editorial Team, London

Donnison, D. and Soto, P. (1980) *The Good City: a study of urban development and policy in Britain*, Heinemann Educational, London

Goffman, E. (1968) *Asylums*, Penguin, Harmondsworth

Hall, P., Gracey, H., Drewett, R. and Thomas, R. (1973) *The Containment of Urban England*, George Allen and Unwin, London

Kreckel, R. (1980) 'Unequal opportunity structure and labour market segmentation', *Sociology*, **14**, 525–50

Martin, R. and Fryer, R. H. (1973) *Redundancy and Paternalist Capitalism*, George Allen and Unwin, London

Massey, D. (1979) 'In what sense a regional problem?', *Regional Studies*, **13**, 233–43

Norris, G. M. (1978a) 'Industrial paternalist capitalism and local labour markets', *Sociology* (12), **3**, 469–89

Norris, G. M. (1978b) 'Unemployment, sub-employment and personal characteristics', *The Sociological Review*, **26**, 89–108 and 327–47

Pickvance, C. G. (1981) 'Policies as chameleons: regional and office policy in Britain' in Dear, M. J. and Scott, A. (eds), *Urbanisation and Urban Planning in Capitalist Societies*, Methuen, London

Chapter 6 The formal urban system

Castells, M. (1977) *The Urban Question*, Edward Arnold, London

Cockburn, C. (1977) *The Local State*, Pluto Press, London

Dearlove, J. (1979) *The Reorganisation of British Local Government*, Cambridge University Press

Dunleavy, P. (1980) *Urban Political Analysis*, Macmillan, London

Ginsberg, N. (1979) *Class, Capital and Social Policy*, Macmillan, London

Gough, I. (1979) *The Political Economy of the Welfare State*, Macmillan, London

Johnson, J. (1972) *Professions and Power*, Macmillan, London

Johnson, T. J. (1977) 'What is to be Known?' *Economy and Society*, 6, 194–233

O'Connor, J. (1973) *The Fiscal Crisis of the State*, St Martin's Press, London

Pahl, R. E. (1975) *Whose City?* (2nd edn), Penguin, Harmondsworth

Pahl, R. E. (1977) 'Managers, technical experts and the state', in Harloe, M. (ed), *Captive Cities*, Wiley

Pahl, R. E. (1979) 'Socio-political factors in resource allocation', Chapter 3 in Herbert, D. T. and Smith, D. M. (eds), *Social Problems and the City*, Oxford University Press

Saunders, P. (1979) *Urban Politics: a sociological interpretation*, Hutchinson, London

Saunders, P. (1981) *Social Theory and the Urban Question*, Hutchinson, London

Supplementary Benefits Commission (1979) *Annual Report 1978*, Cmnd. 7225; and *Handbook*, revised edn 1977, HMSO London

Townsend, P. and Davidson, N. (1982) *Inequalities in Health*, Penguin, Harmondsworth

Chapter 7 Work outside employment

Alden, J. (1977) 'The extent and nature of double job holding in Great Britain', *Industrial Relations Journal* (8), **3**, 14–31

Burns, S. (1977) *The Household Economy*, Beacon Press, Boston

Davidoff, L., L'Esperance, J. and Newby, H. (1976) 'Landscape with figures: Home and community in English society' in Mitchell, J. and Oakley, A. (eds), *The Rights and Wrongs of Women*, Penguin

Fitzherbert, A. (1958) *The Boke of Husbandry*

Gershuny, J. (1978) *After Industrial Society? The Emerging Self-Service Economy*, Macmillan

Gershuny, J. and Thomas, G. (1980) *Changing Patterns of Time Use*, Science Policy Research Unit, University of Sussex, Occasional Paper No. 13

Henry, S. (1978) *The Hidden Economy*, Martin Robertson

Henry, S. (ed) (1981) *Can I Have It In Cash?*, Astragal Books

Illich, I. (1977) *The Right to Useful Unemployment*, Marion Boyars

Illich, I. (1981) *Shadow Work*, Marion Boyars

Meacham, S. (1977) *A Life Apart: The English Working Class 1890–1914*, Thames and Hudson

Pahl, R. E. (1981) 'Employment, work and the domestic division of labour' in Harloe, M. and Lebas, E. (eds), *City, Class and Capital: new developments in the political economy of cities and regions*, Edward Arnold

Rule, J. (1981) *The Experience of Labour in the Eighteenth Century*, Croom Helm

Thompson, P. (1977) *The Edwardians*, Paladin Books

Wallman, S. (1979) *The Social Anthropology of Work*, Academic Press

Ward, C. (1977) *The Child in the City*, The Architectural Press

Chapter 8 Approaches to urban power

Castells, M. (1977a) *The Urban Question*, Edward Arnold

Castells, M. (1977b) 'Towards a political urban sociology' in Harloe, M. (ed), *Captive Cities*, John Wiley

Cockburn, C. (1977) *The Local State*, Pluto Press

Crenson, M. (1971) *The Un-Politics of Air Pollution*, Johns Hopkins Press, Baltimore

Davies, J. G. (1972) *The Evangelistic Bureaucrat*, Tavistock

Dearlove, J. (1973) *The Politics of Policy in Local Government*, Cambridge University Press

Donnison, D. (1981) *Cities in Trouble*, University of Glasgow, Centre for Urban and Regional Studies, Discussion Paper No. 39

Dunleavy, P. (1980) *Urban Political Analysis*, Macmillan

Hall, P., Gracey, H., Drewitt, R. and Thomas, R. (1973) *The Containment of Urban England*, Allen and Unwin

Harloe, M. (1975) *Swindon: a Town in Transition*, Heinemann

Lambert, J., Paris, C. and Blackaby, B. (1978) *Housing Policy and The State*, Macmillan

Lukes, S. (1974) *Power: a Radical View*, Macmillan

Marriott, O. (1967) *The Property Boom*, Hamish Hamilton

Newby, H., Bell, C., Rose, D. and Saunders, P. (1978) *Property, Paternalism and Power*, Hutchinson

Newton, K. (1976) *Second City Politics*, Oxford University Press

Pickvance, C. G. (1977) 'Marxist approaches to the study of urban politics: divergences among some recent French studies', *International Journal of Urban and Regional Research*, 1, 219–55

Saunders, P. (1979) *Urban Politics: a Sociological Interpretation*, Hutchinson

Williams, O. P. (1971) *Metropolitan Political Analysis*, Free Press, New York

Young, K. and Kramer, J. (1978) *Strategy and Conflict in Metropolitan Housing*, Heinemann

Chapter 9 Conclusions

Centre for Contemporary Cultural Studies, University of Birmingham: (1976) *Resistance Through Rituals*, Hutchinson; (1979) *Working Class Culture*, Hutchinson; (1980) *Culture, Media Language*, Hutchinson

Hoggart, R. (1958) *The Uses of Literacy*, Penguin

Illich, I. (1978) *The Right to Useful Unemployment*, Marion Boyars

Pahl, R. E. (1983) 'Concepts in contexts: pursuing the "urban" of urban sociology' in D. Fraser and A. Sutcliffe (eds) *The Pursuit of Urban History*, Edward Arnold

Saunders, P. (1981) *Social Theory and the Urban Question*, Hutchinson

Szelenyi, I. (1981) 'Structural changes of and alternatives to capitalist development in the contemporary urban and regional system', *International Journal of Urban and Regional Research* (5), 1, 1–14

Williams, R. (1961) *Culture and Society*, Penguin

Williams, R. (1965) *The Long Revolution*, Penguin

Willis, P. (1977) *Learning to Labour*, Saxon House

Sources

Statistical data providing evidence on the processes and structures of urban life can be found in a number of government and other publications. On housing, the following are particularly valuable: *Social Trends* (annual), the decennial Census of Population, and the *National Dwelling and Housing Survey* (1979). Data have been collected together in *Housing Policy: Technical Volume* (1977) published by the Department of the Environment. *The Department of Employment Gazette* publishes monthly data on the labour market and unemployment and this is summarised in the Manpower Services Commission's *Labour Market Quarterly Reports*. The Chartered Institute of Public Finance and Accountancy publishes annually data on spending by individual local authorities on different services.

INDEX